SAMMY

ALSO AVAILABLE

Brainiac by Justin Vellucci

De La Soul by Dave Heaton

AFI by Andi Coulter

Fountains of Wayne by Fiona McQuarrie

Laughing Hyenas by Steve Miller

The Apples in Stereo by Josh Bloom

SAMMY

Jeff Gomez

J-Card Press

COPYRIGHT © 2026 BY JEFF GOMEZ

All rights reserved. This book or any portion thereof may not be reproduced or used in any manner whatsoever without the express written permission of the publisher except for the use of brief quotations in a book review.

ISBN 979-8-9917394-4-3 (print)
ISBN 979-8-9917394-5-0 (ebook)

Library of Congress Control Number: 2026935144

J-Card Press
460 Center Street #6578
Moraga, California 94570

Designed by Monte Karp

www.jcardpress.com

To RS, who liked them first

When you quit, you quit, but you always wish
You knew it was your last shot

—Lou Reed

CONTENTS

OPENING CREDITS | 1

1: WHATEVER HAPPENED TO YOU ON THAT STREET? | 15

2: WHATEVER HAPPENED TO YOU IN THAT CLUB? | 89

3: WHATEVER HAPPENED TO YOUR OLD GUITAR? | 181

END CREDITS | 219

CHAPTER NOTES | 221

OPENING CREDITS

The nineties were filled with bands that disappeared. Groups who either burned out brightly or simply faded away after a record or two. Even the biggest band of the decade, Nirvana, only released three albums and was around for just a handful of years. That was, of course, an extreme case, with a tragic reason behind the short career, but the group's duration wasn't atypical for the period. Several acts from the alternative era put out just a few LPs before calling it quits. Whether disbanding officially or just sort of fading away, plenty of groups who began the decade weren't around by its end. The list is long, even if the lifespans were short.

Nirvana's huge success may have had something to do with this. In the alternative era, stakes were high. Labels, always looking for the next big thing, wanted results fast. When or if big sales didn't come, bands were dropped. It wasn't like the seventies, when boutique operations like Asylum or the newly created Geffen Records nurtured talent and allowed or even encouraged artists to grow over time. Back then, albums that sold poorly didn't necessarily end careers. The nineties were different. The resulting shock and disappointment were enough to cause some disheartened groups to just break up, ending it all rather than go back to an indie or small label.

It was impossible for fans to know what had happened to these groups. In a period before the internet, unless the breakup was covered in *Spin*, *Alternative Press*, or a smaller, regional publication like *Flipside*, ardent or even casual admirers had no way to learn the details of why or how bands they liked didn't last. This sometimes led to rumors getting passed from person to person at rock clubs or record stores. You were likely to hear tales of a major-label deal gone sour, a front man in the depths of drug addiction, and so on.

Without solid news, all there was to go by was the music (or lack thereof). A fan would go to a record store and look for a new release by a band they liked: an album, EP, or just a single. Any sign of life. Or else they'd scan the local free alternative weeklies looking for the group's name in the listings of upcoming shows. After a few years of searching, and finding nothing, you just kind of figured out that it was over. The band was done. But what had happened? Where did they go? Why did it all end? Some fans became obsessed by a band that vanished. For me, that band was Sammy.

I first heard Sammy in 1994 when I was living in Los Angeles. I was driving home from somewhere. It was evening, around eight or nine. Too late to be coming home from work, too early to be coming home from a date. The radio was tuned to KCRW. What came out of the speakers was a song I didn't know but instantly liked. Trebly guitar, shuffle beat, a bit off-kilter all around. Then the vocals kicked in. "Rudy, it's getting late. You just assumed that I ain't got no date." The sneer and the language were pure New York. There was Lou Reed in the lo-fi. And I liked Lou

Reed, a lot. This was right up my alley. I bopped my head along to the song as if I'd been hearing it my whole life, and yet I'd never heard it before—didn't even know who it was—and the tune wasn't even more than halfway through. "You and me, we worked the same bar. We've come a long way, but it's not very far." Funny too.

Soon enough I was pulling into the skinny driveway that led to a small wooden parking garage behind a series of bungalow apartments in Larchmont Village, right near the gate to Paramount Studios. Up in the hills was the Hollywood sign. I would see it grow larger and larger every time I drove north toward the apartment, and it'd get smaller and smaller in my rearview mirror every time I drove south. Very LA.

I parked the car, a cheap old BMW nearly as old as I was, and waited for the song to finish and for the DJ to tell me the name of the group. I sat there for three more tunes, a bit more than ten minutes, until I heard the name Sammy.

On my next trip to Aron's Records, I bought Sammy's debut album. It was on a small label and, back then, I liked things on small labels. I thought that made the music sound better. An EP followed, and a year or so later, Sammy put out another record, *Tales of Great Neck Glory*, this time on Geffen. I bought it all. I loved it all.

Why did Sammy hit so hard? What spoke to me so much that night in the car? After all, in that period of my life I was a sponge, constantly soaking up new sounds and bands and scenes. I haunted every record store in LA and saw shows all over town, from concert venues like the Palladium and Palace to tiny holes-in-the-wall like Jabberjaw and Spaceland. I was even in a band myself, playing guitar and writing songs. So I knew a bit of the DNA of both the creation of tunes and what it meant to be in a room with other people to make a *sound*. So why and how did Sammy rise so high above all the rest, to the point where—here I am now, more than three decades later—still listening to (and now writing about) them?

What appealed to me most were Jesse Hartman's lyrics. *That's* what drew me in. Yes, the music was great: jangly Fender-powered lo-fi indie rock with just the right amount of ironic swagger. But what made Sammy run was Jesse's words. Luke Wood's musical backing and instrumental ideas were of course integral to the sound, and his business acumen and connections were surely hugely important in organizing the attendant chaos that comes from being a group—not to mention that Sammy was aided over the years by other musicians who fleshed out their songs—but Jesse's contribution was outsized. He was both the beating heart of the band and its brain.

What Sammy's lyrics gave me were stories; the songs created scenes in my head. It was like I was watching a movie, and yet I was listening to a record. How did Jesse do that? The words provided pictures, and my imagination made those scenes move in a simulacrum of cinema. When I would later learn that Jesse was himself a filmmaker, that made a lot of sense. It explained the construction and effect of many Sammy tunes.

What I also liked about the lyrics is that they were literary. Not in the sense that the songs were wordy or self-consciously artsy; Jesse was no Gen X Van Dyke Parks. Instead, he was Raymond Chandler mixed with Raymond Carver, penning hard-boiled tales about lovable losers.

This resulted in tunes that had a beginning, middle, and end—songs that could stand on their own as discreet, and complete, moments in narrative time.

All of this went against the grain of the nineties. Back then, it was fashionable for songs to be short and surreal, to not give a fuck. Sammy wasn't like that, and a big reason why was the words. You cared about these songs because they were about people—characters with tics, behaviors, voices; you could almost picture them existing outside the song, escaping its confines like Jeff Daniels's character in *The Purple Rose of Cairo* and sidling down to Odeon or Nell's for a drink. In "Snow Is Falling in Manhattan," David Berman writes, "Songs build little rooms in time." Sammy built an entire world, inhabited by two-bit gangsters, suburban dreamers, riot grrrls, Long Island boys, and a dozen others. A universe constructed so solidly it still stands today. When I sat on my couch all those years ago and listened to *Debut Album*, it was like Rudy and all the rest were in that small apartment, sitting right next to me. And when I reach for those records now, all those characters circle and swirl around me once more, old friends I'm glad to see again.

Back in the day, I didn't know much about the band—I never saw, let alone read, an interview or magazine article about them—but from looking at the liner notes, I knew it wasn't a group in the typical sense. Sammy was just two guys: Jesse Hartman, the singer and lyricist who played rhythm guitar, with Luke Wood on lead guitar. They wrote the tunes together and fleshed out their sound with a variety of assorted musicians and rotating drummers, none of whom I knew. This meant Sammy was kind of like a Gen X Steely

SAMMY

Dan, except the music wasn't jazzy, and the songs were short and mostly devoid of solos. I'd even figured, even though there was nothing to suggest this, that—like Steely Dan—Sammy had begun at college with two like-minded friends getting together to make music. (This would later prove to be correct; Jesse and Luke met while attending Wesleyan, a mere hundred miles away from where Walter Becker and Donald Fagen assembled at Bard.)

I lived in Los Angeles for most of the nineties, and saw Sammy there twice. Once at the Roxy, opening for Teenage Fanclub, and later playing with That Dog at Las Palmas Theatre. At that second show, my friends and I managed to get backstage. I met Luke and told him a story about what had happened when I saw them at the Roxy; he was friendly.

But as the decade went on, and finally closed out—the nineties dead-ending into a new century—there was nothing else from Sammy. Just silence. No new records. No more gigs. And no word about what had happened. Not that I was completely preoccupied with the group. There was plenty going on in my life to distract me—new relationships, a burgeoning writing career, a cross-country move from Los Angeles to New York—but still, every once in a while, I'd think to myself, *What became of those two guys?* These thoughts would hit me at the most random of moments: stuck in traffic, riding the subway, brushing my teeth. *Sammy. What the hell happened?*

As the years passed, the fact that the group was just Hartman and Wood only deepened the mystery. There weren't four or even three guys to wonder about. It was just Jesse and Luke. This gave me both more and less to ponder.

Getting ghosted by a band is not unlike getting dumped in a relationship. The object of your affection is no longer around, but you still like and think about them. Mutual love that was once alive and reciprocated now becomes a one-way street. Obsession can easily creep in. When it's a person, we pine for and miss them. When it's a band, we still privately cheer and clap, but increasingly into an abyss. These absences ultimately leave holes in our lives. Albums become more like snapshots, a moment in time, literal records. Sometimes they're even hard to listen to, like good memories that turn bad because they were *too* good. They ferment into something else; what had been joyous discovery gives way to bittersweet repetition.

It didn't help that my history with Sammy was wound together with an old girlfriend I'd met again at one of their shows. High school sweethearts, we hadn't seen each other in years. When we met as seniors, she was very feminine, dressing in Laura Ashley and wearing her hair long. That night on Sunset Boulevard her hair was cut short and dyed purple. She had a pierced eyebrow and purple lipstick that matched her thatched hair. She'd gone full indie chick. "What are you doing here!?" she'd shouted over the band when she saw me. We were on the floor at the Roxy, Teenage Fanclub blaring in the background. Shouting back, I replied, "I came here to see Sammy!" It was true. I liked Teenage Fanclub well enough, but I liked Sammy more. She just shook her head and gave me that grin I used to love. "No, *I'm* here for Sammy." After an embrace, she shouted into my ear, "Who did you come with?" Most of my friends were into harder stuff—Sonic Youth, Fugazi, Jesus Lizard—so I was at the show alone. When I told her this, she answered, "Then you're coming home with me."

We dated for a while, but it broke apart for the same reasons it did the first time around. We were different people, even more so after high school. We stayed friends, but as the new decade dawned and I moved to Manhattan, we drifted apart. I never heard from her again. When I'd think of her, I'd think of Sammy. The fact that they'd similarly disappeared made it even more strange. Whenever I tried to learn about either the group or her, I came up empty. What had happened to her? What had happened to them? After being in New York on 9/11, and seeing both towers fall with my own eyes, I began to ask larger questions: What was happening to our country? What was happening to the world?

When I later saw a copy of the second record by Laptop, Jesse Hartman's solo project, in an East Village record store, I right away recognized the Sammy singer on the cover. I was shocked. It was like seeing a face on the street I'd only seen on milk cartons under the headline MISSING. I bought *The Old Me vs. the New You* there and then and played it as soon as I got back to my apartment on Avenue B. I was instantly perplexed by the album's overall computer sounds and crooned vocals. Where were the guitars? Where was that voice? This did *not* sound like Sammy. Around this same time, I'd heard somewhere that Luke Wood, the other half of Sammy, was an industry big shot working behind the scenes. Both developments signaled to me the twists and turns that life can take. Not that I needed much reminding. My own life around that time was beginning to transform in ways I hadn't imagined.

I'd moved to New York to be a writer. Some early success—two books published by a major publisher in just a couple of years—made it seem like that was maybe going to happen. I moved to the Upper West Side and began to jog in Central Park. I had season tickets to the opera, subscribed to

New York and *The New Yorker*. I dated difficult but beguiling women. Artists. I started to see my life unfurling in front of me as a Woody Allen film: I'd spend Sunday mornings with *The New York Times* and a couple of bagels. A few cigarettes and some strong coffee. Evenings would be spent meeting friends for drinks, a bite to eat; then we'd see where the night took us.

As time went on, things began to change, as did my whole idea of myself. My writing career sputtered out, but I got a job in publishing and began to rise through the ranks. I met a great girl and we got married. Then we had a kid. The kid was great too. My career flourished. It was all different, but somehow better than what I'd imagined. Better than what I had thought I wanted. I was beginning to realize how much people could change, and how so many things could happen to one person, in one life. And yet, over the years, as I reached for those Sammy records, I still wondered where they'd gone, what had happened to them.

An early hero of mine had been F. Scott Fitzgerald. While I liked his writing, I liked his story more. How he'd had it all and then lost it all. Where he'd once been paid thousands for a short story in the twenties, fifteen years later he was groveling to editors for a few hundred bucks for his Pat Hobby tales, sketches about a failed screenwriter that were bitterly autobiographical. My first novel was even issued by his first publisher, Scribner. When it came out, there were ads for Scribner's new paperback line, which I was a part of, with my book featured next to some of Fitzgerald's. It was a bizarre combination, and one I knew I was not worthy of.

In an essay from *The Crack-Up*, published in 1945, five years after he died at the age of forty-four, Fitzgerald wrote, "I once thought that there were no second acts in American lives." I was beginning to see that there were. My own life was proof of that. When I would extend that thinking outward, looking for more examples in different people, I would often return to Sammy. It was the biggest mystery I could recall from the nineties. Had they had second acts? If so, what did they entail? Where did they end up? What had happened?

Thirty years after buying *Debut Album*, I had to find out.

I started by looking for Jesse and Luke online in early April 2024. I secretly hoped I wouldn't find them. The vision I had in my head was that I was embarking on an adventure, a quest. I wanted this to be hard. I wanted to search for clues, go down rabbit holes, face dead ends.

Based on the brief bits I knew about the band, Jesse lived in New York and Luke lived in Los Angeles (at least, that's where they'd been in the nineties; who knew where they were now?). I'd lived in both places over the decades but was now based out of Northern California, in a small town not far from Berkeley and Oakland. The words ROAD and TRIP began to form in my mind. I quickly made a mental list of old friends I would look up when I flew to Manhattan as I sought out Jesse. How many bagels would I eat? How many slices of pizza?

I quickly found email addresses for both Jesse and Luke and penned an introductory note that included both a truth and a lie. In the short message, I said I was a fan who was just curious why I couldn't find any Sammy stuff on Spotify—neither of the records, and the EP was also missing. Of course it was true I was a fan; the lie was the reason for why I was writing. I was trying to see if either of them would answer, and if they did, find out how they felt about their old band. For all I knew, Sammy was a sore subject, something they'd each sworn to never discuss again. Maybe there'd been some great rift between them, and those records and songs were something to be forgotten rather than celebrated. Perhaps I'd be opening old wounds. Perhaps I'd get yelled at. Or maybe I'd encounter only silence.

Jesse wrote back the very next day. With a somewhat trembling hand, I clicked on his reply. Jesse thanked me for writing and told me he was trying to sort out the streaming situation. Seeing as how he seemed open to the general idea of discussing Sammy, I figured I could now take things to the next step. I wrote him back and told him I was a writer and that I wanted to write a book about his old band. The only hitch was, seeing as how Sammy was essentially a duo, I had to have the story from both perspectives; Luke would need to be involved too.

After I sent the email to Jesse, I let out a deflated sigh. It looked like I wouldn't be going to New York after all. *Oh well*, I figured. *There's always Luke.* I then had visions of catching a Southwest flight to Burbank, renting a car, and driving the streets of Silver Lake, armed with a copy of *Tales of Great Neck Glory*. I would prowl the streets and reservoir, pointing to the CD and asking shopkeepers, hipsters, and dog walkers, "Have you seen this man?" Jesse quickly put an end to that idea as well. He informed me that he was still friends with Luke, they talked all the time. He'd check with him about the book idea and get back to me. *Damn*. A few weeks later I had my answer: They were both interested.

We set up a Zoom toward the end of May to talk about the project. I made a short presentation to walk them through my thoughts and approach to the book I intended to write, the story I wanted to tell. They were each cool with the concept and seemed generally bemused, if not slightly touched, that a stranger wanted to talk with them about a chapter in their lives they had each considered more or less over. Afterward, they provided a few email addresses and contact names, and I then went to work with some heavy-duty online sleuthing to find more people associated with the band, and with Jesse and Luke as people.

Over the course of the next year, I reached out to a variety of old friends, producers, and musicians connected to Sammy. I held numerous Zoom conversations with people connected with the group, in addition to having joint and solo sessions with both Jesse and Luke. I also sent questions via email to dozens of associates. Every quote has been taken from either a direct conversation or an email exchange with that person.

Intermittently, I weigh in with my own opinions or views, but for the most part I've done my best to remove myself from the narrative. This is Sammy's story, not mine, so other than this brief introduction, you won't hear from me much.

Is the following true? Is this *exactly* what happened? Well, the truth can be an elusive thing. What's true to me may seem false to someone else, and in an age when our political reality, not to mention even the most mundane facts, which had long been settled, appears to be up for debate (flat Earth, anyone?), it's easy and tempting to drive yourself crazy deciding, let alone defending, what's real and what's not.

What follows in the ensuing pages is my own take on

what transpired as cobbled together from the stories and recollections long buried in the thoughts and memories of those involved. Keep in mind that much of the story takes place thirty years ago, if not even farther away. I doubt anyone I contacted thought I'd come along and ask these questions. I didn't think I would either. But then I did.

Here's what I was told.

1: WHATEVER HAPPENED TO YOU ON THAT STREET?
Growing up, high school groups, leaving home

F. Scott Fitzgerald began work on his most famous novel, *The Great Gatsby*, while living in the small Long Island community of Great Neck, New York. He moved there in the fall of 1922 and stayed until leaving for France in the spring of 1924, which is where he completed the book. Settled by the Dutch in the seventeenth century, Great Neck is a well-to-do community of small villages and hamlets located just a few dozen miles from Manhattan. In this quaint town of leafy tree-lined streets, with charming names like Pond Road, many of the area's palatial homes are mansions on the water complete with docks, boats, shallow beaches, and amazing views. As a peninsula bordered by Long Island Sound, Fitzgerald used Great Neck's odd topographical shape—Manhasset Bay creates two communities that face each other—to create the fictional East and West Eggs in his novel. He lived in Kings Point, the "West Egg" of *Gatsby*'s geography.

About a mile from where Fitzgerald wrote *Gatsby*'s opening chapters is the neighborhood of Strathmore. This is where Jesse Hartman grew up. Unlike the more storied and monied areas of Great Neck, Strathmore was middle-class. Here you might find divorcées and people who had to hold down two jobs just to make ends meet. Plymouths and Chryslers filled the driveways, rather than Porsches and Mercedes, and kids from Strathmore were more likely to go to a state school than anywhere Ivy League. It was all pretty much the opposite of Kings Point. Jesse lived in Great Neck until he went away to college. Even after graduation he returned to the area, literally and metaphorically. Portions of Sammy's first LP were recorded at the house of an old friend who lived just up the street from where Jesse grew up, and Sammy's second and final album, *Tales of Great Neck Glory*, was a poisoned love letter to the town.

Jesse Samuel Hartman was born in March 1969. His family, including two older siblings who were already teenagers—a sister and brother who'd been raised in Old Bethpage—had moved to Great Neck in 1968. Jesse's parents were both teachers at nearby high schools. His mom taught in Plainview while his dad taught in Glen Cove. His mom later ran the math department at two schools, while Jesse's dad oversaw the social studies department at North Shore High School. "They were both powerful and respected in their own universe," Jesse says, "but in the grand scheme of things, in affluent Great Neck, if your parents were high school teachers, you felt like you were from the wrong side of the tracks."

The biggest change since the era of Fitzgerald was the influx of increasingly diverse families and ethnicities. "Great Neck was like Wakanda for Jews," Jesse says. "It was the ultimate spot." Most of the parents had been born in Brooklyn but moved to the suburbs for the sake of their children. "The way I look at it, it was Brooklyn 2.0," says Michael Corn, Jesse's childhood friend and future musical collaborator. "Everyone's dad was from Brooklyn. They all wanted something a little better for their families and, if they could afford it, Great Neck is where they went."

Even though Jesse's parents chose the town for its idyllic setting and the good public schools that came along with it, they were not content to be just suburban people. In fact, one of the reasons they chose Great Neck was its proximity to New York City. Manhattan was just a thirty-minute train ride away on the Long Island Rail Road, a.k.a. the LIRR. When he was growing up, his parents took him to the city every chance they could to visit museums or attend a show. Jesse not only continued this habit when he got older and could make the trip on his own or with friends, he wrote a song about it. On the Sammy B-side "L.I.R.R.," he sings to a girl named Linda:

Want to meet me at the station
Dressed so pretty
Yeah, we can hop on the train
Go through the tunnel to New York City

From his parents' perspective, it was a perfect situation. They had the safety of the suburbs, while being close enough to the city to reap its cultural benefits. Everything seemed great. "Jesse was a well-rounded, talented kid," remembers Michael Corn. "He was good at sports, he was popular. He liked music. He had his foot in all the worlds going on." But for Jesse, it was harder than it looked. "I was always running in these circles," he remembers, "but I always felt a little bit unlike a lot of the kids I was around." He was not unlike *The Great Gatsby*'s Nick Carraway, the outsider who lived in the shadow between two mansions and wryly observed the worlds of both West and East Egg without properly belonging to either. As Carraway states in the book, "I was within and without, simultaneously enchanted and repelled by the inexhaustible variety of life."

Years later, Jesse would use his memories of not quite belonging to great effect, writing biting and satirical songs about Great Neck and the people he knew there. But that was all in the future. For now, as far as anyone knew, he was just another Strathmore kid. "I went to the right summer camp, took the teen tour to Israel. All the things the wealthier kids were doing." All of this on the salary of two high school teachers. "I don't know how they did it," he says. "When I look back on it, I'm kind of amazed and impressed by what my parents pulled off."

The sacrifices his parents made, and the opportunities they created, would later change the entire trajectory of Jesse's life. "I guess they were inadvertently putting me in a position to meet someone like Luke."

A six-hour drive northwest from Great Neck is Rochester, New York. One of America's first boomtowns, the area exploded in the nineteenth century after the Erie Canal was completed, opening the region (and much of the country) to expansion, commerce, and new industries. By the twentieth century, Rochester was a bustling metropolis boasting two colleges, the University of Rochester and the Rochester Institute of Technology, as well as the Eastman School of Music. And because it was home to companies like Eastman Kodak, Xerox, and Bausch & Lomb, the area became a nexus for science, engineering, and technology.

This is where Luke Foster Solberg was born in February

1969. Eighteen months later, his father abandoned the family, which also included a sister, Martha, who was six years older. "He went off and married the golf pro at the Monroe County Golf Club," Luke says. "He was not involved in my life and didn't want to see me. He just wasn't engaged and had no interest in being a father. He wanted to go and find his new life. So, it was just me, my sister, and my mom."

Luke skiing in New York, 1973. Courtesy of Luke Wood.

It was a typical story in many respects. Fueled by the pill and changing attitudes about sex, in the seventies the divorce rate in America climbed to 50 percent. And while the emotional trauma of divorce was hard enough on kids and spouses, there was often also an accompanying economic hardship. Millions of women were suddenly single moms, thrust into the workplace and forced to support themselves and their children. It wasn't always easy. Even though much of it is silly, the 1980 screwball comedy *9 to 5* shows what working women were up often against in the Me decade: rampant misogyny, sexual harassment, unequal pay.

After her divorce, Luke's mom got a job as a social worker, working in pretrial and diversion programs, helping defendants get assessed for substance abuse and wellness issues. She did this all through Luke's childhood. She would go on to oversee Monroe County's entire pretrial and release agency.

In the early seventies, there weren't great childcare options for working parents, especially for parents with younger kids (fifty years later, things haven't changed much). Luke's only option was to attend two different preschools on the same day. His mom would drop him off at the first preschool at nine. He'd be there until noon. The second preschool lasted from one until his mom picked him up after work. The problem was getting from one preschool to the other. As a five-year-old, Luke couldn't be expected to walk or take the bus on his own. What ended up happening was the principal of the first school volunteered to drive Luke to the second school in her own car. During the ride, the car radio was always on. As Luke remembers, "That's where I first fell in love with pop music." On any given day he'd hear AM radio staples like Paul Simon's "50 Ways to Leave Your Lover" or "Wildfire" by Michael Martin Murphey. "These are songs that, to this day, I remember as being magic to me coming through these speakers."

As a child, Luke had always been by his mother's side, and now she was gone all day and he was alone, surrounded by strangers. The tunes coming out of those tinny speakers helped fill the gap and soothe the trauma caused by the divorce. "I felt really alone. And music made me feel not alone." For a while, those rides between schools were the only place where Luke would hear that music. Even though his mom liked music and had sung in choirs—once traveling all the way to Germany to perform—no music was heard in the house. "She was too busy being a working mom," Luke says. "There was no leisure time for her. She was just trying to get from A to B and not have her life fall apart."

The third track on the fourth record by the Velvet Underground is called "Rock & Roll." The song tells the story of Jenny, a five-year-old whose life is transformed when, one morning, she tunes into a New York radio station and has her life altered by the music she hears. The songs coming out of her radio provide an instant escape from parental problems and the crass chasing of consumer products she sees all around her. As the first verse ends, Lou Reed sings, "You know, her life was saved by rock and roll." The same thing happened to Luke. In music, he says, "I found a sense of community. I found a sense of 'I'm not alone.' I found a sense of soothing." The characters he heard in the songs that played in the car radio became his friends, every track part of an interconnected soap opera that was showing him all the possibilities of what life could be. "The adventures these people are having in these songs," Luke says, "they're so exciting, and they're having so much more fun than I am, but someday I'm going to have that fun too. [Music] really built my sense of identity."

When Luke was six, his mother married a litigation lawyer named Robert Wood. The new family moved to an affluent area in Rochester called Council-Rock Estates, an enclave near four golf courses not too dissimilar to where Jesse grew up, in Strathmore. An ad for the development in 1924 boasted that Council-Rock Estates "offers an abundance of fresh air, freedom, space, charm—an opportunity for enjoying life to the utmost." And if the area's architecture of Tudor, English cottage, and Dutch Colonial homes wasn't a near carbon copy of Great Neck, the idea that moving to the area was good for a person's standing in the community was also the same; the ad quoted above also guarantees that moving to Council-Rock Estates will give families "an invaluable heritage of social approval." When Luke was fourteen, the family moved to the Corn Hill neighborhood, which was near Rochester's courthouse. This ensured that many of the area's inhabitants were lawyers; Robert Wood even had his law offices on the premises, in a suite of offices behind the house.

Growing up, Luke lived the life of a seventies latchkey kid. Alone for hours at a time, and with both parents at work, Luke would spend most of his time listening to music. When he was given a tape recorder, he'd tape disc jockey Casey Kasem's countdown show and play it over and over. His main source for music was the local rock station WCMF, 96.5 on the dial (slogan: LONG LIVE ROCK!). And while he enjoyed the visceral nature of a heavy track like AC/DC's "Back in Black," he didn't emotionally connect with it. The music was still filling a void, but a crucial element was missing.

When Luke was about twelve, his older sister, Martha, began attending Wesleyan University, located nearly four hundred miles away in Middletown, Connecticut. Growing up, she'd been a casual music fan, so Luke was on his own when it came to discovering new bands and genres. But that first trip home for the holidays after an initial semester at school, Martha brought home three cassettes: *Talking*

Heads: 77 by Talking Heads, *Argybargy* by Squeeze, and Elvis Costello's *My Aim Is True*. By this point, Luke was beginning to discover some crossover and college radio fare like the Clash and the Cars. He was also obsessed with "One Way or Another." And even though it was slowly dawning on him that he preferred Blondie over Peter Frampton, he didn't know what that meant. He wasn't connecting these newly discovered groups to any sort of larger or cohesive movement. His sister's trio of cassettes, however, helped place the final piece in the puzzle. Hearing these records, and learning what they were listening to at a liberal arts school, turned on the light bulb in Luke's head. "This is God," he realized. "This is the path." It was the beginning of the young music fan unwinding the string and finding the bridges between bands, and then tying those groups to individual scenes. More importantly, Luke realized that something else came with the contact and inclusion with these subcultures: an identity.

Suddenly, it all clicked. Luke thought to himself, *There's a tribe here I can belong to. And it's somewhere in that world of* Talking Heads: 77. He soon left behind rock station WCMF for good. Instead, he kept turning the dial until he reached the nether regions known as the "reserved band," the area all the way over to the left. That's where you'd find what the FCC termed "non-commercial educational" stations. Located between the frequencies of 88.1 and 91.9, in the eighties these free-form, student-run stations gave birth to "college rock," a loosely defined genre collecting underground bands that released music on independent labels (the Replacements song "Left of the Dial" is a tribute to these stations). What Wood found was WRUR and WITR. First founded as an AM station, the Rochester

Institute of Technology's WITR (89.7) went on the air in 1961. WRUR, run by the University of Rochester, is even older, having debuted way back in 1948. Luke stopped taping Casey Kasem. Instead, he listened to college radio six hours a day. A whole new world was opening for him. And it was alright.

Back in Great Neck, Jesse didn't need college radio; he had his brother. Phil Hartman, who was thirteen and a half years older, was thrilled when Jesse was unexpectedly born. "I always wanted a little brother," Phil says. "I embraced the unlikely opportunity. And Jesse was great from the get-go, though as a late child he was probably a bit spoiled being in his unique situation." Phil and his older sister, Susan, had grown up in Old Bethpage, a town about a half hour from Great Neck. Phil describes Old Bethpage as "much less Jewish, much more down-to-earth" than where Jesse grew up. "Great Neck was great in many ways," Phil says. "Cultured, closer to the city, and so on, but the privilege and homogeneity were pretty hard to take."

In 1974, the summer after his freshman year at Princeton, Phil got a job at a movie souvenir store in Manhattan called Cinemabilia. Also working at the tiny shop were several participants in the just-getting-off-the-ground CBGB scene, including Television members Tom Verlaine and Richard Hell; Terry Ork, the group's manager; and Robert Quine, who would later play in Hell's post-Television group the Voidoids as well as with Lou Reed. Also working there was David Bowler from the four-piece power-pop band Marbles (not to be confused with an English duo active in the sixties named the Marbles). Although Phil became friendly with

Richard Hell later, at this point the only one he hung out socially with was Bowler.

As a die-hard music fan, Phil threw himself into the scene. He saw Talking Heads the second time they played CBGB, and he was there the first time Television played Max's Kansas City (opening for Patti Smith in the days before Smith was backed by a full band). Phil was also buying all the cool records of the day, and when he went away to school, he left some of those LPs at the family home in Great Neck. "He had every record you were supposed to have at that time," remembers Jesse. Bowie, Iggy, the first Ramones album. Jesse spent hours in Phil's room. "As a kid, I was always fumbling around in there, reading his diaries and looking at the posters on his wall." Every square inch was covered with film and music posters. "It was like a little museum I always had access to." The Sammy song "Encyclopedi-ite" is all about Phil and his influence on Jesse; its opening lines even speak to Jesse's adolescent cultural explorations: "I used to sneak into your room / Felt like I was raiding King Tut's tomb." When friends would come over, Jesse showed them the room and forced them to read lyrics off record sleeves. Most were unimpressed.

As a kid, Jesse was originally into what everybody else his age in Great Neck was into—the Beatles, of course—but also Barry Manilow, Boston, Lynyrd Skynyrd. As he puts it, "Shit that was floating around the kids' scene." When those records would appear at home, at first Phil would gently tease Jesse about them. Then he took a more active approach, consciously guiding his brother toward the good stuff. "It was a little hard to make mistakes," Jesse remembers. "He would catch you before you could make your mistake. He wasn't going to let me go too far down any paths, whether it was heavy metal or show tunes." One day, the brothers were shopping for records. Phil was pulling down from the shelf PIL's *Metal Box* as Jesse was busy thumbing through the Ozzy Osbourne section. Phil caught sight of this and put the Ozzy album back. As Jesse says, "He was definitely pushing me." Some LPs threw Jesse for a loop, such as Captain Beefheart's *Trout Mask Replica* and *The Modern Dance* by Pere Ubu. "He had things I didn't totally get until later." The earliest memory Jesse has of getting his older brother's approval was when he bought the debut album by the Cars. "That's when I first bought something that I liked that he could accept."

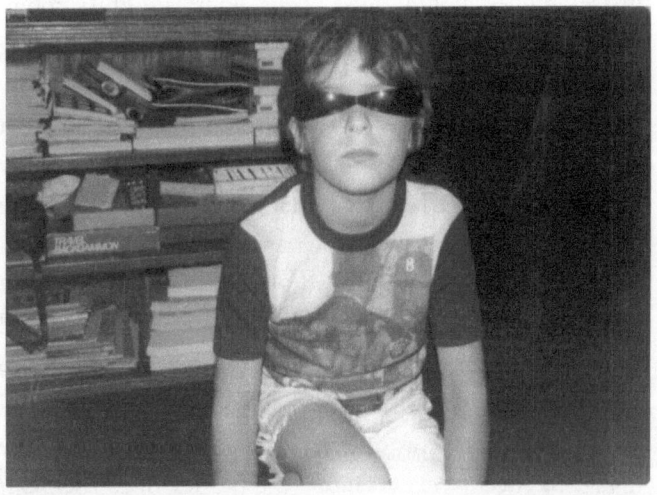

Jesse, age seven, on July 4, 1976, at a bicentennial party in Great Neck. Courtesy of Jesse Hartman.

Jesse was soon leaving behind Barry Manilow and getting deeply into hipper stuff like Talking Heads, the Human League, Gang of Four, and the Mekons. He then tried to introduce these sounds to his friends and other people his age. When he went to camp at the age of ten, he brought with him a mixtape that Phil had made for him. While other kids were playing Michael Jackson's *Off the Wall*, Jesse forced his fellow campers to listen to Gang of Four. Back at home, he did the same thing. His cheerleader girlfriend from elementary school came over for a date, and Jesse picked as make-out music Gang of Four's LP *Entertainment*. "To me, that was my world," he says. "I was very confident with it. It seemed like the right thing. I was almost like proselytizing to other kids about this stuff that I was learning about."

Phil's strong influence was not without its downside. Jesse would wonder, especially as he got older, how much of his personality and path in life were the products of his own decisions or how much had been guided by Phil. "I was in a box of coolness," Jesse says. Sometimes that box felt constricting. "There was a lot of push and pull inside of me." He went back and forth, embracing Phil's influence while also trying to escape its strong gravity. Later in life this would manifest itself in big geographical leaps; Jesse tried leaving New York and living in Los Angeles. He considered moving to Europe. "It was always a bit of a fight within myself between a kid that really worshipped his older brother and needing to kind of figure things out on my own." Jesse wondered, *Am I a musician because of him, or is it really in me?* "That was always a question I would ask myself. But now that I've grown up, and I've had my own kids, I can see, no, that's not why I'm doing what I'm doing. It's quite the opposite. You pursue the things you really do want to do yourself. Sometimes there's a little bit of a spark that kicks you along, but no one's going to turn you into a singer of a rock band if it's not inside of you."

Not to be outdone by Phil, Jesse's older sister, who was already gone for college by the time Jesse arrived, also played a significant role in a couple of artistic milestones.

SAMMY

Susan Hartman got an MFA from Columbia and took a job teaching in Winter Park, Florida. During these years she was also a writer. Copies of her poetry books—*Dumb Show, El Abogado*, and *Satyr*—were in the Hartman house in Great Neck, and Jesse read them. He would also go to her poetry readings. When Jesse was nine, he visited her in Florida, taking a plane by himself. While down there, he went to book parties in fruit orchards populated by professors and friends of his sister who had names like Wyeth Wyeth. "She wasn't as influential as my brother—nobody could be, really," Jesse says. "He made it his mission to be that for me—but yeah, Susie was impactful." It was Susan, not Phil, who first took Jesse to CBGB. As the epicenter of New York punk, and the home base of so many legendary groups that Jesse loved, the club loomed large in his imagination. The bar happened to be about a block from where Susan was living after she moved back to town. Once, when Jesse was visiting, and they were walking by with Susan's boyfriend Ben (who's now her husband), she said, "Let's go in." Onstage performing was Big Fat Pet Clams from Outer Space, a group that released only one record, but it was notable for having been coproduced by CBGB owner Hilly Krystal. Even though he was only in the club for a few minutes, the place made a big impression on Jesse.

Having a cool older brother and sister made Jesse feel like he had two sets of parents. His mom and dad fulfilled the traditional roles: they were members of the "Greatest Generation" and the children of immigrants; they had good, honest jobs; and they taught Jesse solid values. But his older siblings turned him onto cool stuff and showed him perhaps another way to live his life: as an artist. Having access to so much culture also meant Jesse wasn't the usual bored kid from the suburbs. "I always had an escape from Great Neck," he says. Music, film, poetry, it was all at his fingertips.

But there was more to Jesse's listening habits than just post-punk and the downtown New York City scene. In the sixth grade, he got into the Doors, big-time. It started with the *Greatest Hits* LP and snowballed from there. And while Phil had a couple of Doors albums in his collection, they weren't a favorite. Whereas, for Jesse, something clicked. "The Doors were a big deal for me," he says. The band even ended up playing a big part in his first musical performance.

While Jesse was busy getting schooled in the ways of film and rock and roll by his siblings down in Great Neck, up in Rochester Luke was finding a kindred spirit who would prove to be his musical partner in crime. Hugh Flynn, whose dad was a professor at the University of Rochester, lived in the nearby suburb of Brighton. Both Hugh and Luke were students at the Allendale Columbia School, a private prep school sandwiched between two country clubs. They met the summer before sixth grade when their moms dragged them to a school fundraiser. Each had brought their bike, so rather than just hang around watching their parents work all day, they rode around together on the dirt paths behind campus. "By the end of that afternoon," Flynn remembers, "I had made a new friend. For the next six years we would be inseparable."

Luke and Hugh quickly discovered they shared the same taste in music, a rarity at the ritzy school where students had to don jacket and tie. "It was an exciting time for music in Rochester," says Hugh, "and we were not about to miss any of it if we could help it." In addition to its two college radio stations, Rochester was also a stop for national touring bands. Most groups would play the city as part of the live circuit, hitting Rochester and sometimes Buffalo in between concerts in larger local markets like Boston, Toronto, and New York. Luke remembers, "Everything went through Rochester back then."

The pair's first show, which they saw in April 1983, when they were in ninth grade, was U2 at the Rochester Institute of Technology. The band was on the road supporting their third studio album, *War*. The concert took place at the school's hockey rink, which was occasionally converted into a venue for rock concerts and other performances. After the show, to wait for their ride, Hugh and Luke made their way downstairs to where the locker rooms sat next to a parking lot. It turns out they'd given Hugh's dad a pickup time that was well after the end of the show, so the building was mostly deserted. Until it wasn't. As Luke and Hugh were standing there, U2 appeared and began to do some waiting of their own. They were expecting Richard Butler, lead singer of the Psychedelic Furs, to pull into the parking lot. Butler's band had played the night before in Buffalo. The teenagers couldn't resist the chance to speak to their heroes. "I have no memory of what we said to them," says Hugh. "But I do recall Luke engaging Bono in conversation, while I had something of a brief chat with the Edge and Adam Clayton." Hugh's dad showed up before Richard Butler did, and the high schoolers drove home giddy from the experience. Decades later, when Luke was firmly ensconced in the business side of the music industry, he became friendly with Bono and the Edge. He reminded them of their discussion that night in the locker room below the hockey rink, but they didn't remember him.

From that night on, Luke and Hugh did everything

they could to see live music. Luke's parents would handle dropping the duo at the venue, while Hugh's dad would pick them up, sometimes as late as two in the morning. For professionals with nine-to-five jobs, it was less than ideal, but all the adults could tell what music meant to their kids, and so sacrifices were made.

A favorite for Luke and Hugh during these formative years was R.E.M. Luke loved absolutely everything about the Southern band's artsy, spiritual, romantic music. The first time the pair saw the group live was when R.E.M. played in nearby Henrietta as part of the Little America Tour. The Dream Syndicate was the opening act. Luke and Hugh got to the venue at three o'clock, and when the doors opened at six, they rushed to the front of the stage. There were no barriers between the crowd and the band, so Luke and Hugh were pressed right up against the monitor wedges, a foot from the performers. Even though the pair loved R.E.M., they were equally psyched to see the Dream Syndicate; their record *Days of Wine and Roses* had been a formative album for Luke, helping him to master rhythm guitar. When a heckler next to Luke got out of hand, Steve Wynn threw a beer at the rowdy concertgoer but hit Luke by mistake. "[Steve] then came back and apologized to me and gave me towel," Luke remembers. "I kept the towel for several years."

A year later, just as Luke and Hugh were finishing up summer jobs in the kitchen of a girls' camp in New Hampshire, Luke persuaded his mom to take them to a show just over the border in Portland, Maine. R.E.M. by this time was touring for their *Fables of the Reconstruction* album. Hugh recalled, "It was a great show and a great way to end the summer." The pair also saw the band on subsequent tours for albums *Lifes Rich Pageant* and *Document*. At the show supporting *Document*, with 10,000 Maniacs opening (singer Natalie Merchant will soon make an appearance in these pages), a funny sequence of events led to R.E.M. lead singer Michael Stipe asking Hugh for *his* autograph rather than the other way around. (Stipe did it to politely remove himself from some fans who had him cornered; Hugh was only too happy to comply.)

In addition to being a destination for larger bands passing through town, Rochester had its own vibrant and varied music scene. Local groups such as Absolute Grey, the Chesterfield Kings, Personal Effects, the Colorblind James Experience, Invisible Party, and many more played local halls and bars. Luke and Hugh tried to catch as many of them as they could. Absolute Grey was a particular favorite. Their cover of the Velvet Underground's "I'm Beginning to See the Light" put Lou Reed on Luke's radar. Similarly, the Chesterfield Kings exposed him to the sounds of *Nuggets*-era garage rock, while another local act, the BBBs—with their Beatle boots and cool haircuts—impressed with covers of sixties classics like "Steppin' Stone" and "Gloria."

The drinking age at the time was eighteen, and some clubs were lackadaisical when it came to checking IDs, so occasionally Luke and Hugh could bluff their way into a show. The big club in town was Scorgie's, on Andrews Street in downtown Rochester. As a two-level establishment housing a bar upstairs with a rocking jukebox and live music downstairs, Scorgie's was a combination of CBGB and Max's Kansas City. National and local punk and new wave acts played there (Elvis Costello was reportedly thrown out one night in 1983). Sometimes Luke and Hugh managed to sneak in, but most nights they didn't. Says Hugh, "Scorgie's was the toughest place to get in for those under eighteen." As an example, when Paisley Underground act Rain Parade passed through Rochester in 1984, they played Scorgie's. Luke and Hugh had no luck getting into the show. When the band returned in 1987, Scorgie's had closed, but the friends saw Rain Parade at Idols, a local dance club that had opened around the corner. Seeing all these groups triggered something inside Luke. "That was it for me," he remembers. "I was like, *I want to do that.*"

Even though Luke and Hugh were seeing a lot of great live music in their hometown, Luke still felt he was missing something. He wanted more information about the bands he liked. He wanted to learn about where they came from, who their influences were. Luke knew he'd have to seek out these answers for himself, and he figured he'd find them in New York City. The problem was, the subway didn't stretch from Rochester to Manhattan, and by car it was a nine-hour drive. But Luke wasn't going to let a little thing like geographical distance deter him. For nineteen dollars he could buy a plane ticket from his hometown to NYC on People Express, a no-frills budget airline. On one of his trips, while he was shopping in the legendary bookstore the Strand, Wood came across a paperback of *Uptight*, the short history of the Velvet Underground written by Victor Bockris and Gerard Malanga. "It was like the book of secrets," Luke remembers. Not only did it fill in his gaps of knowledge concerning one of his favorite bands, but it also named writers and artists who had inspired Lou Reed: James Joyce, Kafka, Dostoyevsky, Rimbaud. Names Luke had never heard. He marked them with a highlighter and then went to the library and got books by them all. (On one of his trips to Manhattan he also bought a fake ID on Forty-

SAMMY

Second Street. Seeing as how the ID consisted mostly of his own handwriting in blue ink, it's no wonder it failed to get him into Scorgie's.)

During all of this, Luke continued to log countless hours listening to college radio. One day, when he heard the WRUR DJ give out a phone number and ask people to call in with requests, Luke obliged. He then began dialing the station every five or ten minutes. After a while, he tired of deluging disc jockeys with song suggestions, and instead asked a question. "How can I come work there?" Upon being told that he could come in to apply to be an intern, Luke hopped on his bike and rode over (the campus was about five miles away). Even though he was sixteen and looked even younger, the station manager assumed Luke was a student at the university (Luke certainly didn't volunteer that he wasn't). The unglamorous role of an intern was explained to him: you do chores, you clean up, you sort records.

On his first official day of work at the station, Luke was introduced to the "free pile." This was the stuff that nobody wanted, LPs by acts that were considered too weird and uncommercial even for college radio. Rifling through the stack of castoffs, he came across *Sound of Confusion* by Spacemen 3, the band's debut album that had been released that July. Peering at the Halloween-orange cover, Luke liked that one of the band members resembled Lou Reed. He pulled it out and took it home. The English band's two-chord psychedelic stomp sounded to Luke like the Stooges influenced by the Velvet Underground (which made sense since one of the tracks, "Little Doll," was in fact by the Stooges). He couldn't believe such a great album was in the free pile. "I was so confused," he says. "I was like, 'Why are you throwing this record away? You should be *playing* this record.'" He ended up loving the LP so much he returned it to the station and resubmitted it for consideration, pinning to the sleeve a long and passionate recommendation. A week later, when he was back at the station doing his normal rotation of chores, he ran into the music director. The director thanked him for having pushed the station to give the Spacemen 3 record a second look. *Sound of Confusion* was indeed going to be added to the playlist. Luke was happy, but not satisfied. He didn't just want to work at the station; he wanted to be on the air.

When Luke asked how he might make the transition from cleaning bongwater stains off the couch to playing records, the music director recited a litany of hurdles that would have to be vaulted to make this wish come true. It seemed to Luke like a lot of stuff. Too much stuff. While he was contemplating all this, Luke noticed a list on the wall entitled TEMPS. "What's that?" he said. The music director explained that Christmas was coming up, and with so many students leaving town, the station needed temporary help to keep the station running. Sensing an opportunity, Luke volunteered to be one of the temps. It worked. After a brief bout of training, they let him be a fill-in DJ.

Luke finally had a public outlet for his passion, a way to show the depth and breadth of his musical taste and knowledge. And he reveled in it. In the span of a typical show, he'd play foundational bands like the Ramones and the Clash in addition to rarer punk rock gems like "Streets of Saigon" by Bloody Mannequin Orchestra and 9353's "Famous Last Words." He did so well during the holiday season that, the following year, he was given his own show. Wood, by this time all of seventeen years old, called his show

SAMMY

The Athens Hour and all he played were bands from Athens, Georgia, the small college town that birthed acts such as B-52s, Pylon, and, of course, his beloved R.E.M.

With every layer of the musical onion being peeled, Luke was getting closer and closer to the center of the thing he loved. One final step remained: to make music of his own. To do that, he'd need to learn how to play an instrument. Or, at first, a tennis racket.

Jesse's first instrument was piano, which he began at the age of seven. He learned the basics from a few teachers who came to the house, where Jesse would play on the family piano in the living room. He began taking lessons when he was eight from Arnold Friedman, a retired teacher who also taught computer classes. In the basement of Friedman's modest home on Piccadilly Road, a line of Commodore PET 2001 computers sat on top of collapsible tables in front of metal folding chairs. The family even had a red Volvo station wagon with the personalized license plate COMPUTER. "At the time, he was the best piano teacher in the neighborhood," says Jesse. "He was a well-regarded person and teacher. A lot of people took lessons from him." Jesse would visit the Friedman home for the next four years. While there, he'd sometimes see Friedman's son Jesse, who was the same age and who went to the same school. One afternoon, when Jesse's mom came to pick him up after a session, she was alarmed to find her son sitting on Arnold Friedman's lap. At that time, it didn't seem like anything more than a momentary lapse. A few words were exchanged, but the lessons continued. Years later, the incident would take on a decidedly more sinister feel.

Jesse's parents were supportive of his playing and would often sit on the couch and listen to him pick out Beatles tunes from a fake book. The first rock song he learned to properly play was "Riders on the Storm" by the Doors. Jesse was in the sixth grade and heading for his bar mitzvah. Seeing as how Great Neck was a predominantly Jewish population, not to mention one with so many kids around, there were lots of bar mitzvahs to attend. Each one was a lavish affair held in a catering hall with lots of food and live music. And with so many kids attending who knew how to play an instrument, it became routine for youngsters to sit in with the hired band for a song or two. As Jesse's bar mitzvah approached, his plan was to play an instrumental version of "Riders on the Storm" with the band. In the weeks before the big event, Arnold Friedman taught Jesse to play the haunting tune.

When the day finally arrived, Jesse was looking dapper in a dark three-piece suit and tie, his brown hair feathered in a popular eighties style. Sitting behind a Crumar T1/C electric keyboard, he began to play the Doors classic. "Everything was going fine until the first chorus," he recalled. It turns out, all the band knew was the first part of the tune. When Jesse started playing the next section, the band stayed with the first part. "They didn't change, but I was changing." Despite the small snafu, the performance, and the afternoon, was a big moment for Jesse. "The bar mitzvah itself is a musical experience," he says. "It's forcing you to practice a whole bunch of singing, and you get up in front of people."

With the bar mitzvah behind him, Jesse switched from piano to guitar. He had his eye on joining a band, and he didn't think keyboards was very rock and roll. But he didn't know where to start. Even though his older brother was a

SAMMY

huge influence in terms of listening to music, when it came to making music Jesse lacked a mentor or direction. He also didn't know of any cool kids in the neighborhood to advise him on what brand guitar to buy, or what kind of pedals you might need to make your amp sound not so clean. "I didn't have a mentor in that way until I met Luke," Jesse says. He and his dad went to a Sam Ash music store in Long Island and bought a white Japanese-made Westone Strat-type model along with a Peavey amp. Not the most cool or hip choice, but it got the job done. His first guitar teacher was a Pete Seeger type who taught Jesse folk songs meant for an acoustic guitar. In no time, however, Jesse was learning songs by the Meters and Jimi Hendrix. He still would play piano occasionally, but he never took another lesson.

Up the hill from Jesse lived Michael Corn, who was the same age. The two were never especially close, but they'd been going to school with each other their entire lives. Seeing as how Corn played piano, performing stuff like Billy Joel songs at elementary school assemblies, everyone in Strathmore knew how good he was. Even though Jesse, in those days, hated Billy Joel, he eyed Corn as someone he could start a band with. Corn had started playing piano at the age of five. Musical ability seemed to run in the family: Corn's mom played piano (and painted), his aunt also tickled the ivories, while his grandfather strummed a guitar. Although Corn's father was a doctor, a profession that was commonplace in an upper-class area like Great Neck, their livelihood was still a struggle. "Even though we were in this neighborhood that was pretty well-to-do," says Corn, "my dad was kind of just getting by, even with a successful private practice."

In middle school, Jesse and Corn formed a group along

with a mutual friend, Ivan Nass on bass, and Corn's good friend Michael Cohn on drums. The name of the group was Rough Edges, a name chosen by Corn. "Much to my dismay," says Jesse, who was never a fan of the moniker. It could have been worse. Corn initially wanted to give the name a funky and stylized eighties spelling, something like Ruff Edgiz. "We toyed with that idea at some point," says Corn, "but Jesse definitely put his foot down and was like, 'No, we're not doing that.'" Jesse already disliked the name, so he didn't want to add insult to injury by making it extra cute. The group practiced in the basement of Michael Cohn's house pretty much every weekend. "We got pretty good pretty quick," recalls Corn. "Those were good times."

Jesse brought to rehearsal songs by Hendrix, the Doors, the Who, and the Rolling Stones, if only because he knew his bandmates would balk at edgier material like Gang of Four or the Velvet Underground. "He was always into more artsy music rather than mainstream rock and roll," says Corn of Jesse. "And sometimes divisions would pop up within our band." Those divisions would appear later; for now, the group was gelling. Because Jesse didn't yet have the confidence to put himself forward as the singer, they roped in another school friend, a classmate named Neil. A good-looking early bloomer whose voice had already changed, Neil not only looked the part but also had the pipes to handle the heavy rock songs Rough Edges was making its repertoire.

The band got so good they were allowed to play to the entire school as a special assembly. This was made possible by the fact that the school's principal, Richard Sherman, was a huge fan of classic rock. For the performance, Jesse wore a hip shirt he'd borrowed from his brother. The band was so tight, some students suspected them of lip-syncing to records. Looking back, Jesse says, "It was a ballsy move to force that upon the whole school, to make them sit there for forty minutes." But the students loved it. However, about a week after the assembly, each member of Rough Edges got called to Sherman's office. As Corn slinked away from class, he racked his brain, trying to guess what had gone wrong, and what was going to happen next. *Did we play too loud? Are we going to get suspended?* It was quite the opposite. Instead, the principal wanted to congratulate the band on a job well done. He also presented each member with a special award. By the time graduation rolled around, a few months later, Sherman was still talking about the assembly, to the point where some students in the audience were sick of hearing about it. Besides school, the only other place an underage band in town could play was a space underneath the Great Neck public library called Levels. Levels hosted weekly classes, theater productions, art shows, and weekend events. All the programming was chosen by teenagers and was meant for teens. Rough Edges played there often.

As middle school segued to high school, Jesse began to get restless. Sure, he was in a group, but he felt the "cool" factor was missing. Levels was not CBGB, and he was beginning to chafe at some of the material the other guys were bringing in, like Van Halen's "Jump." He began to moonlight in groups with older kids who were more likeminded. One band, Lev Babe Schnozz and the Gang, played "Rock and Roll" and "I'm Waiting for the Man" by the Velvet Underground. The bass player wore a leather jacket and Sex Pistols T-shirts. These were the cool kids. Not content with the underground garage rock of Lev Babe, Jesse also joined a cheesy band called Mirage whose members were into Rush.

"I don't know why I did that exactly," he says. "Maybe I liked the challenge of playing with older kids, or maybe I was flattered to be asked. But at one point I was a member of three or four bands."

Rough Edges on stage at Levels in the early eighties. L-to-R: Michael Corn, Ivan Nass, Jesse. Courtesy of Jesse Hartman.

In between juggling membership in a variety of groups, Jesse also found time to get a job. He worked as a busboy at a popular local restaurant called Millie's Place. In fact, most of the other members of Rough Edges, including keyboardist Michael Corn, also worked there. The fact that Jesse and the other Strathmore kids had to get jobs shows how their parents were trying—and in many ways succeeding—to expose their children to affluence while also instilling in them strong values. "Our parents were working people, and they expected us to work and make our own spending money," says Jesse. "There was no allowance. We were on our own to figure things out." The restaurant opened in 1977 and was named after the owner, Millie Gubbins. The decor and feel of the place were very seventies, with philodendrons, brocade, tapestries, and fringed lampshades filling the space. Diners sipped on California chardonnay as Steely Dan's *Aja* played on a loop in the background. The restaurant seated 160 people, and even though a review in the *New York Times* when it first opened described the food as "consistently mediocre," all those seats were constantly filled. Waiters wearing suspenders and red bow ties zoomed through the dining rooms, while would-be diners crowded in the small waiting area up front (Millie's Place did not take reservations). "The customers were crazy," remembers Jesse. "The staff was nuts."

One employee that Jesse and the others befriended was a Bruce Springsteen/John Cougar–type rocker with slicked-back hair named Louie Max. Max, who was a decade older than Jesse and his friends, played shows in Manhattan performing under the names Louie Maxx and the Streethearts, Louie Maxx and the Heart Attacks, and, later, the Corner Boys (he dropped the extra "X" around 1991). Jesse and the others would go see him perform. Jesse, by then a budding songwriter, offered his services to the older musician. Max took him up on the offer, traveling to Jesse's house, where they sat at the family piano in the living room working on songs. It was a sort of trial run for an experience Jesse would have years later when he collaborated in a similar fashion with an even older, and much more prominent, musician.

Jesse's employment at Millie's was wacky and a lot of fun, but it wasn't the dark and sinister side of life he was hearing about in so much of the music he liked. He also felt cheated because it hadn't always been this way. In the seventies, Jesse's brother Phil witnessed demonstrations against the Vietnam War in front of North High. But by the time Jesse was a teenager, the biggest controversy in town was the rivalry between ice cream outlets Baskin-Robbins and the newly introduced Häagen-Dazs. Occasionally, however, glimpses of Great Neck's seamy underbelly would appear. In the ninth grade, Jesse's science teacher was found stabbed to death in his garage, murdered by a young male prostitute he'd met in Manhattan. "One day," Jesse says, "he just didn't show up for biology class."

By far the biggest scandal to rock the town involved Jesse's former piano teacher, Arnold Friedman. In 1987, after federal agents discovered a large collection of child pornography in the Friedman home, Friedman and his son Jesse were arrested on numerous charges of sexual abuse. They both each later pled guilty to sexually abusing several kids who had been to the home as part of Arnold Friedman's computer classes (events which are chronicled in the documentary *Capturing the Friedmans*). The case broke the summer after Jesse went to college, and when he came home for Thanksgiving, it was all anybody in Great Neck could talk about. "A lot of cases of the kids that were victims were younger than me," says Jesse. "So whatever happened there, happened after my time there. I got lucky." Michael Corn, who didn't take lessons from Arnold Friedman, once attended a bar mitzvah where Friedman was the hired entertainment. Corn stood by as Friedman played, waiting for an opportune moment to ask if he could play something. At one point, in between songs, Friedman turned to Corn and screamed at him, "Get the fuck out of here!" Bewildered, Corn went to the kid whose bar mitzvah it was and relayed what had just happened. The kid then told his mom, who was a psychiatrist, but the woman just waved the complaint away, saying that Friedman probably had had too much to drink but was otherwise harmless. In the wake of the allegations and stories that came to light after the arrest and trials of the Friedmans, it seemed that everyone in Great Neck had similar stories. "It was really fucking upsetting," recalls Jesse. "It was the ultimate *Blue Velvet* kind of moment." As he began to make the transition from playing cover songs to writing his own material, what Jesse heard and saw all around him began to make an appearance in his music.

The first instrument Luke played wasn't an instrument at all. As a kid, he was obsessed with the Blondie song "One Way or Another." To jam along with his favorite track, he took a Dunlop tennis racket and fashioned a strap out of one of his dad's ties. He'd strum the racket over and over while he sang the song, doing his best rock star moves in front of a mirror. When he became a teenager, he wanted to play the real thing.

Forty minutes south of Rochester was Geneseo, New York, home to Buzzo Music. Located on Main Street, and run by a kindly trumpeter named Al Bruno, Buzzo's stocked instruments as well as records. The walls of the small shop were plastered in posters and record sleeves, while a corkboard sported MUSICIANS WANTED notices written on index cards. When Luke wandered in to get his first guitar, he was talked into buying an Electra X-260 for $295. They told him it was the best and cheapest guitar they had on hand. It looked a bit like a Les Paul. Luke bought it, but he wasn't happy, then or now. "In retrospect, it's interesting because it's the least culturally connected instrument you could start with," he says. "Nobody played this guitar. Maybe it looked a little like Jerry Garcia's guitar, but I hated the Grateful

Dead." Within a year Luke had upgraded to an Indonesian-made copy of a Fender Stratocaster. It was better, but he still wasn't satisfied. He'd since become obsessed with getting a Rickenbacker because that's what R.E.M.'s Peter Buck played.

Once he owned a proper instrument, Luke eschewed lessons, choosing to pick up chords here and there from friends or learn by ear from records. On one of the nights he and Hugh Flynn successfully snuck into a club, Luke met Chaz Lockwood, a local musician six years older who played with bands around town such as Lotus STP and Invisible Party. Lockwood played a Strat and was an adept musician. When Luke asked for advice on how to play, Chaz (real name Charles) told him to listen to Television, Big Star, Richard Thompson, and the Neil Young LP *Everyone Knows This Is Nowhere*. All of it proved the perfect syllabus for the young guitarist. In no time, Luke could play the long solo in "Marquee Moon." As he began to master the instrument, Luke was also figuring out what kind of player he wanted to be. He knew he didn't want to be a flashy virtuoso in the mold of Eddie Van Halen.

For Luke, it was less about the precise notes than about the chordal movement in the song, the underlying structure, the elements that made it a *song*. He then began to learn how to rearrange chord progressions from existing tunes to make something new. For example, if he learned a song whose chords were G-D-C, Luke would alter that slightly, playing G-C-D and continuing to change the sound and the shape of the tune until he had a song of his own.

When he was fifteen and in California on a trip with his stepdad and mom visiting his stepbrother, Luke came across a Rickenbacker in a shop that was being offered at a fair price. He talked his mom and stepdad into buying it for him and returned to Rochester with the new guitar. This is what he played all through high school. With his dream instrument finally in hand, now all he needed was an amp. The day he went shopping for one, he had to decide between two models, a new Peavey Bandit 65 or a 1968 Fender Twin Reverb. The Fender was a monster; when Luke picked it up, it felt like it weighed eighty pounds. He went back and forth, back and forth, trying to decide. In the eighties, the idea of a "vintage" instrument didn't exist; there was only new gear or old gear, and old gear had the same cachet as a used car (which is to say, not much at all). But Luke went with his gut and chose the Fender. "It was the first good decision I made in my music career." He has the amp to this day.

Once Luke had a real guitar, knew how to play, and began writing his own material, the next logical step was to form a band. The first person he recruited was his best friend, Hugh Flynn. Not only did it make sense because they already had similar musical tastes and got along well, but seeing as how Hugh had played both trumpet and baritone horn in elementary school, he had a basic musical foundation upon which to build. Flynn made his own trip to Buzzo's and bought a red Electra X-630 bass for $260. He began taking lessons from Oliver Brown, the younger brother of Absolute Grey lead singer Beth Brown. For ten bucks a week, Oliver came to Hugh's house and gave him lessons. A big fan of Paul McCartney, Oliver taught Hugh not just the basic major and minor scales but also a bit of Beatlesque song structure. "With a small number of lessons, a small amount of music theory," says Hugh, "and an even smaller amount of training in songwriting, I was ready to get started." Seeing as how Hugh had a bass but had not yet purchased an amp, he and Luke would jam in Hugh's bedroom with the bass hooked up to a Technics stereo. The next step was to find a drummer.

Through their copious concertgoing and attempts at nightclubbing, Luke and Hugh were familiar with a punk rock kid in town named Richard Ford (given that he sported a foot-tall mohawk, he was a hard guy to miss; also, this was a different Richard Ford from the Pulitzer prizewinning novelist, though I'm sure a mohawk would have looked good on him too). Ford suggested his older brother, Dave, who played drums. Dave attended a prep school down the road from where Luke and Hugh went. The Harley School was a bit more artsy, with a theater program and a big emphasis on art and music. The school also skipped having uniforms and ties.

Like any newly formed band, now all they needed was a place to practice. Hugh had the perfect solution. Behind his family home was a small carriage house that doubled as a garage and physics lab for his academic father. Set back from the street, and with solid twelve-inch walls, the racket the young group would make was unlikely to disturb neighbors. Just as important, Hugh's dad had installed a furnace, so the space was kept warm and toasty through the cold Rochester winters. For the next three years, this would be the band's home base.

At first, progress was slow. Luke struggled with barre chords, and Hugh was still mastering the blues scale. Of the three, Dave Ford was the most musically proficient. But soon they began to gel and produce something resembling music. More importantly, the trio was having fun. Practices produced informal jams, general goofing around, and

SAMMY

learning songs by other bands. They made playing a gig their goal. "It's funny looking back at it now," Hugh recalls. "We believed we could do it, so we did. Either that, or the idea that we couldn't do it never seemed to occur to us."

In their first incarnation they were a hardcore group. The reasons for this were twofold: it was music they liked that was easy to play, and they drafted in uber-punk Richard Ford to be their singer. Luke's thought at the time was *I've got Glenn Danzig in my band: I'm good.* For two months they fashioned themselves in the mold of Black Flag, the Dead Kennedys, and Suicidal Tendencies. Now they just needed a name to match. One arrived on a hot summer day. Luke, Hugh, and Dave were grabbing food in a nearby park when Luke, commenting on Dave who had taken off his shirt due to the heat, described his hairy and sweaty band member as a "Nehru-zombie-looking motherfucker." Hearing this, Hugh suggested Nehru Zombie as a band name. It stuck. To the group, the moniker had a kind of retro-kitsch B-movie vibe, the same as the Cramps, the Misfits, or 10,000 Maniacs. What didn't stick was the commitment to being a hardcore group. After two months, Richard Ford left the band and Nehru Zombie transformed into a neo–Paisley Underground act, with Luke as the singer and a sound indebted to their heroes R.E.M. As a bridge between the two influences, Nehru Zombie would perform a jangly cover of a Circle Jerks tune.

In no time they started playing out, opening for popular local groups like Absolute Grey and Invisible Party. Nehru Zombie performed at industrial dance club Scrap, a neighborhood bar called Rumors, and Idols, the venue where they'd seen the Rain Parade. The place they played the most was Jazzberry's.

Nehru Zombie flier for local show. Courtesy of Hugh Flynn.

Opened in 1984 as a vegetarian restaurant, in addition to hosting bands for all-ages shows, Jazzberry's also held poetry readings and theater pieces. And despite their success in clubs and bars, Nehru Zombie performed at any and every house party they could find. "Hell," says Hugh, "we even played birthday parties." To spruce up their stage show, they drafted in a friend to provide a light show like the Velvet Underground's early gigs when they were still under the tutelage of Andy Warhol. Their work quickly paid off. Nehru Zombie soon had their own following, playing to up to four hundred people. "Rochester had a very supportive environment and scene," says Luke. "One of the gifts for me in what I did later in my life was being in a place where you could play and have a stage, but it wasn't serious, it wasn't a major market." The town was the perfect combination of being large enough to make an impact, but not so large as to be insurmountable or intimidating.

For Luke, it was an easy decision about what to do next.

Jesse was ready to make a similar shift from being in a cover band to playing originals. It began the summer after tenth grade when he went on a teen's trip to Israel. While he was away, he wrote his first song, "Standstill," cowriting the lyrics with another kid. By the end of the summer, he had a handful of compositions. Over that same summer, Rough Edges keyboardist Michael Corn was having his own musical awakening. As he got interested in more complex musical forms (such as jazz fusion), he took up drumming. Almost overnight he became proficient. It was good timing since tension had crept into the band, stemming from musical differences, much of which came from their current drummer, Michael Cohn. "Our drummer was into Genesis and arena rock," says Corn, "and Jesse hated this stuff. Michael would say, 'Let's do a Genesis song,' and Jesse was like, 'No way, we're not doing that.'"

Everything came to a head one school night when Jesse was at Corn's house to work on a song he'd written. Cohn was supposed to come over and play drums, but he never showed up because he had to study for school. "It was becoming more and more apparent that he wasn't going to be available to do certain things that we wanted to do when we wanted to do them," remembers Corn. He stepped behind the drums, played, and that was it. The new band became Jesse singing and playing guitar, Ivan Nass on bass, and Corn on drums. The only problem was that Cohn had been one of Corn's best friends, and his removal from Rough Edges created a rift. "We talked about it as best we could as kids, being thirteen, fourteen years old, but he was pissed about it." The relationship never quite recovered. "It wasn't the nicest thing to do," says Corn, "but that's the way it went down." To make a clean break from the old group, they decided they needed a new name. They landed on the Sy's, based on Ivan's father's name, which was Seymour (people called him Sy). As Jesse says ruefully, "It was the first in a long line of bad band names." Another development around this time, and which played into the development of the band, was that Corn bought a four-track cassette recorder. Sort of.

In the seventies, home recording meant mastering bulky, expensive, and hard-to-use reel-to-reel machines. In the eighties, new technology introduced gadgets that were small, portable, and relatively cheap, and recorded on standard audio cassettes. The first widely available model was TASCAM's Portastudio. Four-track cassette recorders would go on to revolutionize the way songwriters composed and even how bands recorded, with some groups skipping the studio altogether and making albums at home in their basement or garage (which gave rise to the lo-fi movement of the nineties). Because a four-track was still a relatively expensive piece of gear (at least for a kid in high school), Corn bought it with another friend, and they split the usage of it. The TASCAM would spend a few weeks with Corn before he had to give it up to the friend to use for a few weeks. Corn learned to use the TASCAM via a lot of trial and error, and by listening closely to a lot of finely recorded music like Fleetwood Mac, the Eagles, and Steely Dan. The same way he'd mastered the drums, in just a few months Corn was making elaborate recordings of Jesse's new songs for the Sy's. "Corn was a really good engineer," says Jesse. "He was a master at getting a lot out of a little."

A great example of both Corn's prowess on the Portastudio and Jesse's burgeoning talents as a songwriter was the Sy's tune "The Regular." The four-track recording sounds incredibly polished for a trio of kids in high school. Corn's drumming is tight and expressive, Jesse's jangly guitar is intricate, and Ivan's bass gives the song a solid foundation. There's even an instrumental breakdown halfway through the track complete with keyboard stabs, and a guitar solo at the end. This is not the result of tipsy teenagers pressing RECORD and ripping through "Louie Louie." What's even more impressive is that Corn was so new to recording that he didn't know to use a metronome to keep time. He also didn't have Jesse lay down his guitar first so he could play drums to it. Instead, Corn memorized the arrangement and played the drums by himself, to no musical accompaniment except what was in his head, having Jesse only later put down his guitar and vocals over the rhythmic blueprint. That's not the way you're supposed to record a song, but Corn didn't know that.

Just as impressive was Jesse's songwriting and choice of subject matter. "The Regular" was written about customers Jesse had seen at his brother's restaurant in Manhattan. In 1983, Phil Hartman, along with his high school friend Rich Kresberg, opened a small Cajun-inspired eatery on Great Jones Street between Lafayette and Bowery, right around the corner from CBGB. The Great Jones Café was a tiny place, seating only two dozen people. The menu featured items like Louisiana gumbo, blackened redfish, and Cajun martinis (vodka infused with jalapeño peppers). The restaurant quickly became a hub for artists and film people; Jean-Michel Basquiat lived nearby and would hang out often, and director Jonathan Demme married a woman who was a regular.

Phil, Jesse, and Susan Hartman at Great Jones Café.
Courtesy of Jesse Hartman.

Due to its proximity to CBGB and owing to a dearth of other places in the neighborhood, Great Jones Café also became a popular spot for bands to hang out before or after gigs. Jesse went there as much as he could. "My brother owned it," he says, "so for me it was like *Cheers*. I would walk in there with a few friends from Great Neck, and bartenders would call out, 'Jesse!' And then it'd be free drinks." Getting served alcohol while being way underage was cool, but Jesse had another reason to go there. He loved looking at and watching the people who came and went. And while mid-eighties Manhattan wasn't quite as seedy and dire as it was in the cash-strapped, crime-infested, garbage-piling-up "Ford to City: Drop Dead" seventies, it certainly was not the family-friendly destination it is today. Waiters at the Great Jones Café getting ready for Sunday brunch would have to sweep away the empty crack vials from the night before that littered the sidewalk outside the restaurant. This was not the protective bubble of Great Neck. This was real life. In "The Regular," all this manifests in lyrics about paying high rent and fighting with an upstairs neighbor, something a high school kid from the suburbs would not have experienced. There's also a character named Jackie, the first in a long line of protagonists Jesse would name and give life to in song. He croons, "The regular feels at home in the neighborhood." The song is about community, looking for a place to belong. Mature stuff for a sixteen-year-old.

Jesse's other big interest in this period was cinema. Like music, much of it was inspired by his brother. Phil, who had been a film major, sold a few screenplays in the late seventies. One of them, *Bleeding Heat*, a rock-and-roll noir set in Long Island City, became an obsession for Jesse. He spent hours making logos for the unproduced film. Jesse would travel to Manhattan to see independent movies in theaters, while at home he devoured the raw and gritty movies of the early seventies, stuff like *Mean Streets* and the work of Robert Altman and Roman Polanski. He later chose Wesleyan as a college because they had a film program that focused on this period of cinema. Phil even made his own film while Jesse was in high school. *No Picnic* was a low-budget black-and-white movie that later won an award at the Sundance Film Festival for best cinematography (it has recently been rereleased by Film Desk). Jesse hung around the set as much as he could and even scored a few seconds on film (so did Steve Buscemi, whose cameo is credited as "Dead Pimp"). For a while, the Sy's song "Standstill" was going to be on the soundtrack. As much as he loved movies, however, the priorities were clear. Says Jesse, "It was always music first, film second."

As high school began to wind down, the Sy's kept moving forward, writing songs, recording, and playing whenever they could. Same as Rough Edges, they wrangled an assembly and played for their fellow students, except this time it was mostly originals. At their prom, which was held in the city at fancy Park Avenue hotel the Waldorf Astoria, the group even jumped onstage, commandeering the hired band's equipment to bash out the Who's "Can't Explain." Rough Edges drummer Michael Cohn joined them, which was a nice bit of closure for all involved.

The Sy's had one more bit of business before the band members all scattered to college: an audition to play at CBGB. The venerable venue held open auditions on Monday nights. If a group passed, they'd get to open for another band, and if that went well, the group would be awarded its own headlining spot. The Sy's practiced feverishly ahead of their performance. "It was a very intense, nerve-racking experience just taking the stage," remembers Jesse. "You just got thrown up there and had to play for half an hour." Adding to the stress was the fact that his parents, siblings, and assorted friends were all in the audience (including a future member of Sammy). The band played and thought they did well. A few days later, Jesse got the call. They did not pass the audition. The reason? They sounded too much like R.E.M.

In the fall, Jesse reported to Wesleyan University. A liberal arts college founded in 1831, the campus was in Middletown, Connecticut, about a two-hour drive from Great Neck. Even though he'd investigated Brown and Yale, Jesse chose Wesleyan because—in addition to his interest in the school's film program—it seemed like a place where he could continue playing music. "I didn't think I'd find a band at Swarthmore," he says. On his first day, as he roamed around Foss Hill as part of a cheesy orientation event where kids were kicking around a Hacky Sack and playing elephant ball, Jesse spotted a lonely-looking freshman wearing a Velvet Underground *White Light/White Heat* T-shirt. Jesse approached, sat down, and struck up a conversation.

Before Luke could pack his bags for college, he had some unfinished business with his own high school band. Now that Nehru Zombie had a local following, a set of original songs, and a growing confidence, the logical next step was to make a record. When I ask whose idea it was to do so, Luke promptly replies, "It was my idea, I can guarantee you that." Hugh Flynn agrees, saying that even though the group didn't have an acknowledged leader, Luke was always the driving force: "Any gig we played, we played because Luke did the work to make it happen. Recording the EP happened because Luke put the effort and time into finding a studio we could afford and getting the studio time scheduled." To locate a place where the group could record, Luke went back to where it all started: Buzzo Music. On one of the index cards tacked to the wall, he found a studio that charged $150 an hour. The studio was run by Gary Holt and was housed in his country home in Mount Morris, a small town south of Geneseo.

When he wasn't recording local bands, Holt played bass in the Rochester group the Colorblind James Experience. To get a clean and isolated sound for each instrument (which would help when mixing the various sounds together later), and because the band didn't have any experience playing to a click track, Holt had them record live but in separate rooms. Seeing as how the recording was being paid for by Luke's and Hugh's high school jobs (Hugh worked at a hot dog stand, Luke at an ice cream shop), there wasn't space for extensive overdubs beyond some double-tracked vocals and the occasional bit of extra guitar. They also saved cash by enlisting their friend, Gary Smith, who also did their light show and designed their show flyers, to do the artwork.

Nehru Zombie, around the time they recorded their EP. Clockwise: Hugh Flynn, Dave Ford, Luke Wood. Courtesy of Hugh Flynn.

The result was a seven-inch EP with two songs per side. The cover features a moody black-and-white shot of what seems like the pyramids. The band's name is in all-caps at the top, with the EP's title (*Lost and Other Sequential Dreams*) in lowercase at the bottom. The back shows the three band members sitting on stone steps and looking smart in blazers; drummer Dave Ford looks especially cool sporting a skinny black tie and sunglasses. It's an impressive package and listen, especially considering it was made by a high school band.

First song "Little World" features strummed guitar that sounds a lot like the Wedding Present. The vocals are double-tracked on the chorus. On the second track, "Window Pain," Hugh is the star with a chorused bass line that's very New Order. Side 2 opens with "Greater Good of All," a tune that begins with Luke singing plaintively against just a lightly strummed electric guitar. Final track "What's Up" is the outlier, a surf rock rave-up with a Ventures-style guitar solo and long outro featuring guitar freak-outs and bits of conversation (Chaz Lockwood guests on the song, as does the band's friend Mitch Levine). And whereas Jesse's burgeoning songwriting style was leaning toward relaying scenes and creating characters, Luke's lyrics are more straightforward and sincere. Rather than singing about invented people or to a girl he's trying to woo with a simple love song, you almost get the sense that Luke's singing to himself. On "Window Pain" the chorus goes, "Please don't fail me now / I need you more than ever." Even at this early age, Luke was showing the drive and resourcefulness that he'd exhibit—and which would prove so successful—throughout his entire life. He was a guy who not only wanted things to happen but also *made* them happen; this band, and the EP, was just the first example in a long line. What he's singing here is a sort of pep talk to himself. In "Greater Good of All" Luke sings, "You have to look to yourself / That's where all your focus should be." As someone who endured early trauma, and who felt abandoned, Luke quickly learned that if anyone was going to help him achieve his dreams, it was going to be him. There was no use waiting for someone else to come along. The band pressed up five hundred copies of the EP and sold it around town on consignment. They sold almost every copy.

For a while, Luke was satisfied. He'd achieved what all his heroes had done: he'd made his passion real, physical. He could hold his music in his hand. "I felt like I was finally at home in the universe," he says. But in no time, he began to want more. Luke started recording at home, ping-ponging tracks between two cassette decks to create layers of sound. By his junior year, he'd bought his first four-track cassette recorder, a TASCAM like Michael Corn had down in Great Neck. This allowed Luke to multitrack layers of guitar, add reverb, and experiment with stereo panning. He was finally getting closer to the lush sound of bands he loved, like R.E.M. And while they might have lived a thousand miles away, down in Georgia, there was someone a little closer Luke figured he could turn to for advice.

10,000 Maniacs was considered more or less a Buffalo band, and they played in Rochester often. Luke and Hugh had seen the group live several times, and they even had friends who knew various band members. Lead singer Natalie Merchant lived in Jamestown, which was just a couple of hours away. Luke managed to get hold of her home phone number, and one day he sat down and gave her a call. She wasn't home, but he left a message saying he was a musician, he had a band, and he wanted to send her his music. To his surprise, she called him back, leaving a message of her own. At this point, the first 10,000 Maniacs record for Elektra, *The Wishing Chair*, had come out. Merchant was in the midst of finishing the group's follow-up and breakthrough, *In My Tribe*. Since she was not yet famous, Luke figured she was most likely bemused and a little flattered by this brash high schooler.

When they finally connected over the phone, Merchant agreed to hear the band in person, so Nehru Zombie took their instruments and went down to Jamestown to meet her and play. Not content to just get her advice or to meet her in person, Luke asked if she would perform with him. She agreed. Luke sang and played guitar; Merchant harmonized. She then gave him a few ideas about the song's arrangement. She took the band to her rehearsal room and played them a few tracks from the forthcoming *In My Tribe*. Later, at her apartment, Luke remembers seeing proofs of the album artwork lying around. Merchant was incredibly polite throughout, and Luke catalogued the day as another piece of the puzzle that could one day amount to something. And it did. About a year later, the encounter with Merchant helped Luke meet an even bigger hero.

Back in Rochester, in the middle of their senior year of high school, Hugh Flynn—who'd been Luke's musical partner in crime ever since the sixth grade—left the band. Between dealing with serious parental health issues, and falling head over heels into a new romance, he felt it was time to say goodbye to Nehru Zombie. Not wanting to leave his friends empty-handed, Hugh provided a replacement in the form of a fellow student from their school who was eager to join. But by now college was approaching, and Hugh's leaving effectively marked the end of the first period of the band.

In 1987, the year Jesse and Luke reported to Wesleyan, notable albums included Michael Jackson's *Thriller* follow-up *Bad*, U2's mega-selling *The Joshua Tree*, and debuts from Whitney Houston, Public Enemy, George Michael, and Guns N' Roses. The college scene saw the release of Sonic Youth's *Sister*, *Pleased to Meet Me* by the Replacements, *You're Living All Over Me* by Dinosaur Jr., and *Document*, R.E.M.'s final record for an independent label. On the domestic front, the country was deep into Ronald Reagan's second term, the Iran-Contra scandal was dragging into its third year, George H. W. Bush announced his first presidential run, and the stock market crashed that October.

In September, the Wesleyan freshmen gathered on Foss Hill for an orientation mixer. Located between the Foss Hill dorms and the school's football field, the hillside is a slightly sloped expanse of deep green grass dotted with trees. On that day, the new students were playing games and getting to know one another. Luke, however, was sitting by himself wearing his Velvet Underground T-shirt, a trench coat, and sporting what he describes as "a fucked-up haircut." He was decidedly *not* kicking around a Hacky Sack. Watching the bright-eyed freshmen play games and laughing, all Luke could think to himself was *I don't want anything to do with this. I want anything but this in my life.* That's when Jesse approached, sat down, and engaged him in conversation. Within a few minutes, after talking about bands and their own groups, they went back to Luke's dorm room to play music. It was, as Luke puts it, "love at first sight." As someone who had long been a fan of CBGB bands and the New York City scene, Luke envied Jesse's geographical closeness and participation in that world. "He had exposure to things that I was aware of," Luke says, "but they were always once removed." Jesse was similarly impressed. "I'd never met anyone like Luke. He was not Jewish, he was Waspy and very confident," says Jesse, "very much an A personality."

Luke told Jesse about Nehru Zombie, played him the band's most recent demo tape, and mentioned meeting Natalie Merchant. Jesse was impressed by it all. When he heard Luke's music, it was "the most R.E.M. thing I'd ever heard in my entire life. It was boldly R.E.M. It was so R.E.M. you could almost accept it as R.E.M." Considering his own band was denied the opportunity to play CBGB because they sounded so much like the Southern band, sitting there with Luke seemed almost like kismet. Jesse was also impressed that Luke had band photos and had released a record; they'd played real gigs, and not just afternoon shows at a teen center under the local library. This was a guy who had his shit together. When Jesse played a bit of guitar, it was Luke's turn to be impressed. "I immediately knew he was a super-gifted musician," he says. "I could just tell, *Oh, this is a person who has gifts I don't have.*"

Seeing as how Luke already had momentum behind Nehru Zombie—a batch of original songs, a demo tape, the EP—the duo figured the quickest way to be a band was to just continue as Nehru Zombie, at least for a while. For Jesse, this meant returning to the sideman role he'd held in Rough Edges all those years ago. "I think Luke was impressed with my guitar playing," he says, "which was flattering. I never really thought of myself as a lead player. So that's the role I quickly fell into with him." When Sammy got off the ground half a decade later, the pair would switch roles, with Luke playing lead guitar and Jesse singing, something Jesse feels they should have done earlier. "In retrospect," he says, "we should have swapped [those roles] right there." Years after Sammy had ceased operating as a band, and the pair was just hanging out as friends and drinking at a bar in Los Angeles, Luke turned to Jesse and said, "You know, the biggest A&R mistake I ever made was not just making you the singer right off the bat."

Before they could play shows as Nehru Zombie, Jesse and Luke needed a rhythm section. Seeing as how Dave Ford knew all the songs, they kept him on even though he was attending college in Purchase, New York. For a while he made the long drive to Wesleyan for practices and shows. Their first bass player was a fellow freshman who lived in Jesse's dorm named Ben Wheelock. Jesse and Ben had met the previous summer when a mutual friend invited Ben to see Jesse's high school band the Sy's play the CBGB audition. They met up at the Great Jones Café before the show, and Ben and Jesse instantly hit it off. A studio arts major focused on printmaking, Ben was thrilled when he arrived at Wesleyan and discovered that not only was Jesse attending the same school, but he was also living just a few doors down in the freshman dorm (during their sophomore years, Ben and Jesse rented an apartment in town with two other friends). Ben was drafted into Nehru Zombie, even though he was a guitarist rather than a bass player. Since his favorite group at the time was R.E.M., he was at least aesthetically suited to join the group, if only until they found a more permanent member.

The first show the new Nehru Zombie lineup played was opening for a local group at Yale. Nehru Zombie played well, but to a small crowd. An even smaller one greeted their next gig, which was on their home turf of Wesleyan but happened to be an outdoor performance on a rainy day. The band was able to keep dry, but the audience wasn't, so they played to only a handful of people before the gig was cut short due to someone in a nearby dorm complaining about the noise.

Ben was impressed by Luke's drive and his ability to get things done—book shows, write songs, play gigs—in addition to how Jesse and Luke worked together. "I think they were a good collaborative team," Ben says. "I got the sense that they dovetailed well with each other, with Luke having skills and strengths in areas where Jesse was imperfect, and vice versa." Years later, Ben would return to play guitar for Sammy during its final tour, in Europe in 1996.

The next would-be bassist was another fellow freshman. Cynthia Nelson, an English major from Northern California, first met Luke when he came to Nelson's dorm room looking for her roommate. They ended up chatting and striking up a friendship. After growing up playing piano and flute, Nelson had taught herself a bit of guitar in high school but became frustrated with the instrument. At Wesleyan, she had a breakthrough; she could play a bass the same way she'd played flute and piano: one note at a time. Luke loaned her a bass and Cynthia began to practice by playing along to early Cure records. Sometimes she'd practice three to four hours a day. Luke and Jesse were impressed by her growing talent and dedication—the three had begun to hang out together. They gave Cynthia an assignment: keep practicing. If she got good enough, she could join their band.

When spring break arrived, Luke, Cynthia, and two other friends took a road trip to Athens, Georgia. Seeing as how so many bands he admired came from there, he figured he should see the town for himself. "I've always had this infatuation," he says, "with getting as close as possible to the authentic source." None of the travelers had much money, nor did anyone have a credit card, so it didn't take long for the college kids to run low on cash. Once they got to Athens, they walked up and down Broad Street hoping to run into one of the members of R.E.M., all of whom still lived there. Residents were used to seeing the band around town; they were a constant presence at places like the 40 Watt Club, where Peter Buck would jump onstage to play when groups came through town. Despite seeing a few people who *looked* like Michael Stipe (these superfans were known around Athens as Distiples), the real thing proved elusive. Eventually the travelers ran into someone who said, "Oh yeah, Peter just bought a new house on Cobb Street. It's the big one on the corner with the porch." Just outside downtown, the guitarist's huge home was known locally as "Buck Manor." The four college kids drove over. It was around two in the morning. A hearse was parked in the driveway.

Luke climbed onto the huge wraparound porch and looked in the window. What he saw was Peter Buck sitting on the couch with a woman. Bingo! Luke went to the front door and knocked. Buck opened the door. "Peter, you don't know me," explained Luke, "but I'm a huge fan." He then added, "I'm friends with Natalie." He meant Natalie Merchant, who was close to R.E.M. through her short romance with Stipe. And while Natalie being a "friend" was a half-truth, the next thing Luke said was entirely true. "We're out of money and we have nowhere to sleep tonight. Can we spend the night at your house?" Buck, perplexed but intrigued—and perhaps a bit impressed—replied, "This is the weirdest thing that's ever happened to me. Sure." He showed Luke and the others to a guest room upstairs. R.E.M. had recently returned from a tour, so the room was

SAMMY

filled with guitar cases and gear in addition to a lot of books and a piece of art by Howard Finster. Luke couldn't sleep. To be in the same room with all that stuff was too electric, too important, too freighted with meaning. He quietly extracted a twelve-string Rickenbacker from its case and played it for hours. At some point he finally nodded off, getting about two hours of sleep.

Luke woke his friends up around seven. Before leaving, he wrote Buck a long letter, left it on the bannister, and the college kids showed themselves out. More than a decade later, when Luke was making a name for himself in the music business, he was in Seattle. By then he knew Peter Buck a bit through Lenny Waronker because Luke was working with Lenny at DreamWorks and Lenny had signed R.E.M. to Warner Bros. While in Seattle, Luke ran into Buck in a bar. They began to chat, and halfway through the conversation, he brought up the spring break trip from all those years ago. "You won't remember this," Luke began, "but let me tell you this story." He then proceeded to recount the tale of the trip and the house and the porch and the late-night visit. Buck grinned and replied, "Oh, I remember that." The next day, after the group left, Buck had called the band's manager, Jefferson Holt, and told him what happened. Holt was aghast at Buck's hospitality, which he considered reckless and dangerous. Holt called for an immediate band meeting, during which he warned the group that their lives had changed. They had fans now. Rabid fans. Peter told Luke that his unannounced visit had forced the band to think differently about, and indeed even face, their growing fame.

●

Over the summer, back in California, Cynthia Nelson was practicing bass six hours a day. Having mastered the simple but hypnotic bass lines of early Cure records, she now played along to the intricate rhythms of Fugazi and Gang of Four. At night she worked in an Italian restaurant. She practiced so much she developed tendonitis in her wrist. To grant herself a little relief, she'd shove her arm into an ice bin at work where cans of soda were being kept cold. It was painful, but all her hard work paid off. Upon returning to school in late August, Jesse set up a sort of tryout. Wanting to branch out from the Nehru Zombie material they'd played during their freshman year, Jesse and Luke had composed a batch of new songs. These tunes traded R.E.M. jangle for a heavier, proto-grunge sound influenced by Sonic Youth and Dinosaur Jr. Luke and Jesse had also chosen a new band name: Dime Circus. Cynthia played along to the recently written songs, passing the audition.

After practicing with the group every day, sometimes twice a day, Cynthia played her first show at Wesleyan on September 24, 1988 (as she recorded in her journal, "I really enjoyed last night, got a black eye"). More performances followed, including one in December opening for Soul Asylum and another in January where they opened for GobbleHoof, which featured J. Mascis on drums (all night Luke referred to the group as "Gobbledygook").

Mascis had crossed paths before with Luke and Jesse. The first time it happened was in print. In September 1988, Jesse's sister, Susan—who by now had branched out from poetry to journalism—wrote a story for the *New York Times* entitled "For a Few Rock Players, Music Is All in the Family." The article was about how Baby Boomer parents were (somewhat) encouraging their Generation X kids to be in rock groups. The piece leans heavily on contacts Jesse had made and people he was friends with. For example, the mom of his old bass player from Rough Edges, Ivan Nass, is quoted alongside J. Mascis's dad and Cathy Conner, the mom of Gary Lee and Van Conner from Washington's Screaming Trees. Luke's even quoted in the story twice. And while some of the parents openly state that they hope their child's fascination with rock music will be just a phase before settling into a more stable or respectable career, the kids all have a different view. As Luke states, "In 10 years I could be in a management position with a record company." He was wrong; it'd take him only three years.

As that fall turned to winter, having former Nehru Zombie drummer Dave Ford drive to Wesleyan to practice and play weekend shows was becoming an increasingly untenable situation. In his place, Dime Circus went through several drummers. One of the things that made these players not stick around for long was Luke's exacting work ethic and standards. "I was a really hard person to be in a band with," he admits. "I was really ambitious. I thought we'd be on Sire Records. I thought we were really going to do this. And so anybody who wasn't up for that program was going to hear from me." When Dime Circus played Dartmouth College, Luke screamed at one of these temporary drummers for speeding up in the choruses so much the guy quit mid-set.

Jesse, however, had seemingly found a way to make it all work. "I was probably the one person on Earth who could tolerate him," he says of Luke. "And I don't think he'd be offended by that. That was just the reality. He was really intense."

Another thing the band wanted to ditch was their name. A new one soon arrived from an unlikely yet respected source. Knowing that husband-and-wife bandmates Ira Kaplan and Georgia Hubley, from the Hoboken-based group Yo La Tengo, were frequent patrons of Jesse's brother's restaurant Great Jones Café, Luke and Jesse asked Phil to arrange for an introduction and a dinner so they could ask them for advice. All throughout the meal, Luke was hyper-inquisitive, peppering the older musicians with question after question. "We wanted gigs," Luke remembers. "We wanted to know what the secret sauce was, we wanted to know the meaning of life." At one point, when Jesse and Luke were describing their struggle to find a suitable name, Kaplan mentioned that an early idea for his own group had been Worrying Thing. Luke and Jesse instantly liked it and asked if they could use the name. "You want it?" Ira replied. "Have it." Yo La Tengo, which means "I've got it" in Spanish, came from a Venezuelan shortstop for the Mets who played on the team in the sixties. He would shout *"Yo la tengo!"* whenever he chased down balls to not crash into other players. Worrying Thing was an even older baseball reference, going back to something Stan Coveleski, a star pitcher in the twenties, said about the game: "The pressure never lets up. Don't matter what you did yesterday. That's history. It's tomorrow that counts. So you worry all the time. It never ends. Lord, baseball is a worrying thing." After Jesse and Luke used the name for a couple of years, Yo La Tengo brought the phrase back in 1993, naming a track off their album *Painful*, "A Worrying Thing."

As the school year progressed, Cynthia Nelson's tenure in the group was coming to an end. Her wrist was still hurting from all that practice, something she hid from Jesse and Luke (even when they gave her a hard time for not practicing more). She was also beginning to chafe in her supporting role; she began to crave writing and singing her own songs. Moreover, she and Jesse had become a couple, which led to its own set of complications. By early 1989, Nelson left the band. However, she remained friendly with everyone involved, attended many Worrying Thing gigs, and even played bass with Sammy a few times in the nineties.

Jesse and Luke found what would be the Worrying Thing's final rhythm section in another group that had been playing around campus. Tight Stool was formed in 1987 out of the ashes of another Wesleyan band, the Luggage Monks, who'd formed in 1985. Both were trios with Richard Marshall on guitar and vocals, John Steeb on bass, and Tim Orr on drums. Whereas the Luggage Monks was mainly a cover band specializing in playing the songs of new wave and post-punk acts like Talking Heads, Elvis Costello, and Violent Femmes, Tight Stool revolved around Richard's original tunes. Tim Orr describes the band's sound as "super-loud and aggressive and emotional, but in a weird pop way." After getting to know Jesse from hanging around the dorms, both Orr and Steeb (after making sure it was okay with Marshall) joined Worrying Thing.

The new drummer quickly spotted how the musical duo of Jesse and Luke worked, and how their stark differences often proved complementary. According to Orr, Luke "spoke very fast and seemed to be very driven and creatively opinionated. He was smart about the band plotline he wanted. And knew what musical direction he wanted to go in and had a lot of ideas. Jesse was very laid-back, kind of the opposite of Luke, more inward-looking and quiet and easygoing."

The group set to work rehearsing in the practice space they shared with four other bands in the labyrinthine underground of a Wesleyan dorm. And whereas earlier lineups played mostly on campus, this version of Worrying Thing began to book shows farther afield, including gigs in New York City at CBGB and a club on Houston called Downtown Beirut. Things were beginning to happen, but they weren't happening fast enough for Luke. "I wanted to be the real thing," he remembers. "I wanted to make albums. I wanted to speak to the world." A source of frustration for Luke was that he'd already done in high school all the things you're supposed to do in college. He didn't want a slot on Wesleyan's radio station because he'd already had one up in Rochester. And seeing as how Nehru Zombie had played proper shows to hundreds of people, the Friday night keg party that would satisfy most college bands was beneath him. Luke's attitude was *Screw the local party circuit. Let's go to New York City, let's go to Boston.* That's what real bands did, so that's what he wanted to do. "I was a maniac," he laughs. "I was completely off the rails." When I ask Jesse to comment on whether Luke was indeed a maniac during this period, he smiles and replies, "He *was* a maniac, but a good maniac."

Beyond the new rhythm section, another development within Worrying Thing—and one that would have a huge impact on the musical futures of both Jesse and Luke—was Jesse introducing to the band one of his own songs, suggesting that he sing it instead of Luke. "Everglades" (or, as it was known in its early incarnations, "In Filth" or "Filth Glazed") was written after he'd taken a road trip to Florida his freshman year with an older guy from his dorm. It was the first of several visits to the state he'd make in the next couple of years (with this being the first of several songs he'd write about the area). Florida already held significance for him, since he'd gone there as a kid to visit his sister. Performed live as part of a nine-song set on WESU in a show dedicated to local bands, "Filth Glazed" clocks in a minute longer than what would later appear on *Debut Album*. The track starts with a Sonic Youth guitar freak-out before settling into a sludgy, bottom-heavy groove (if Alice in Chains or Soundgarden had written the tune, this is what it'd sound like). Jesse snarls the vocals more than he sings them, at one point shouting "I'm all covered in fucking filth," adding a few seconds later, "that slimy shit." Whenever Luke chimes in on background vocals, he's usually a word or phrase behind Jesse. This version also boasts two instrumental breakdowns that don't appear later. The song was added to the band's set list during the last couple of months of the group's existence and would later serve as the sole musical bridge between Worrying Thing and Sammy.

The summer after his sophomore year, Jesse worked at his brother's new restaurant, Two Boots, a pizza place in the East Village on Avenue A between Third and Second Streets. Founded in 1987 by Phil and his wife Doris Kornish, along with developer John Touhey, the eatery combined the flavors of Italy and Louisiana (thus the name; both regions are shaped like boots). Jesse would work there on and off until he was twenty-six (even after Sammy had signed to Geffen). It was a fun place to work. Besides the famous customers, lots of interesting people worked there, characters and personalities Jesse would later capture in songs.

Among the locals who came into the restaurant, and who lived nearby, was Richard Hell. Born Richard Meyers in Louisville, Kentucky, Hell grew up in the suburbs in the fifties. While attending a boarding school in Delaware, Hell befriended future bandmate Tom Verlaine, who back then was going by his given name of Tom Miller. In 1966, Hell headed for New York City. Upon arriving in Manhattan, he landed a job as a stock boy at Macy's and lived above an Automat. A poet who was heavily influenced by Dylan Thomas, he had early success, getting published while still a teenager in an anthology by the prestigious New Directions press. He also started his own poetry magazine in the late sixties. In 1971, after Verlaine moved to town, the two got an apartment on Eleventh Street between First and Second Avenues. For the next couple of years, the pair would be inseparable. As Hell writes in his 2013 autobiography, "There were lots of things we could say to each other and ways we could behave that no one else we knew appreciated or even perceived." The same year Hell and Verlaine began living together, Hell started his own publishing company. Dot Books released titles by Patti Smith and future literary agent Andrew Wylie. Hell's contribution to Dot was *The Voidoid*, a name he'd use five years later for his backing band.

Hell, inspired by seeing the New York Dolls, pushed Verlaine, who'd been playing acoustic guitar for almost a decade, to go electric and start a band. Hell hesitantly threw himself into the mix. He didn't play an instrument, but Verlaine assured him he could do it, steering him to bass guitar. Verlaine got a friend who played drums named Billy Ficca to come north from Delaware to join what Hell and Verlaine were calling the Neon Boys. Looking for a second guitarist to play against Verlaine, they placed an ad in *The Village Voice*: "Narcissistic rhythm guitarist wanted— minimal talent okay." Among the half-dozen hopefuls were a pre-Blondie Chris Stein and a pre-Ramones Dee Dee

Ramone (then still known as Doug Colvin). Neither got the job. The band rehearsed for months as a three-piece, but never managed to find a fourth member. By the time they hooked up with musician Richard Lloyd, Hell and Verlaine figured there was too much failed history associated with the aborted Neon Boys and chose a new name: Television.

Television was one of the first rock bands to play at CBGB. Soon they would be joined by Patti Smith, Talking Heads, the Ramones, Blondie, and more. Television stood out during this period for having short hair and torn clothes (this was the height of the glam and glitter rock movement). Malcom McLaren, who was hanging out in New York and managing the New York Dolls, loved Hell's look and took it back to England, where he used it as the inspiration for the Sex Pistols. Despite their ad stipulating band members possess "minimal talent," Verlaine soon tired of Hell's rudimentary musical skills. Tension within the band caused Hell to leave the group in early 1975. A week after he left Television, Hell got a call from New York Doll Johnny Thunders. Thunders, along with Jerry Nolan, had left the Dolls and wanted to know if Hell was interested in joining a new band called the Heartbreakers. Hell said yes but quit less than a year later; he needed a group all his own. That fall, the Voidoids played their first show at CBGB.

Phil Hartman had warned his younger brother against Hell, telling him, "Do not go to Richard's apartment. He'll eat you for lunch." But Jesse went anyway, marching up to Twelfth Street carrying a cassette of Worrying Thing's most recent demo. Jesse quickly discovered his brother was right. Hell wouldn't let him up unless Jesse went and bought cigarettes first. After the pack of smokes was procured, Jesse was allowed to climb the five flights to Hell's apartment. Hell played the demo tape and immediately declared he wanted to work with the band. He'd recently run into Chris Stein at a party, and Stein told Hell that if he ever wanted to do music again, or produce anything, he could do it at Stein's Tribeca loft. Hell decided to take Stein up on his offer, with Worrying Thing as his first project.

Worrying Thing, L-to-R: Luke Wood, Jesse Hartman (channeling Richard Hell), Tim Orr, John Steeb. Photo by Cynthia Nelson.

While Jesse was in awe of Hell's place in punk history, Luke was more excited by Chris Stein's connection to Chrysalis Records. It turns out that Stein had a deal with his former label to act as an A&R scout. Says Luke, "To me the prize was, we have a lane into Chrysalis." As a kid he'd strummed that Dunlop tennis racket and sang along to "One Way or Another." Now he had a chance to be on Blondie's label. Jesse borrowed his parents' Honda for the sessions, and he'd stop and pick up Hell and then drive to Stein's loft on Greenwich Street in Tribeca. "It was the craziest apartment you'd ever seen," recalls Jesse. Junk was

SAMMY

everywhere, including World War II memorabilia that included swastikas. Stein walked around in his bathrobe a lot. By this time, he and Debbie Harry were no longer a couple, so any hopes of seeing Blondie's enigmatic lead singer were dashed. Not only that, but Tim Orr, being a huge fan of the group, told Stein how much Blondie's drummer, Clem Burke, had meant to him as a young musician. Stein then proceeded to belittle Burke's skills, saying he couldn't play or keep time, and so on. Orr didn't say much after that.

They recorded three songs: "My Parts," "Silence & Absence," and "Succulent." Luke was the singer, and Jesse played lead guitar. Worrying Thing's sound by this point was heavy, dirty, and very much ahead of its time considering *Nevermind* was still over a year away. If Luke's vocal on "My Parts" was whinier and higher, the song could easily have fit on Dinosaur Jr.'s *Green Mind*, which was released around the same time (Orr's drumming makes the track). "Silence & Absence" is even heavier, with Led Zeppelin drums, prominent bass, and a wah-wah guitar solo; with songs like this, the band could have easily opened for any Sub Pop group and been called back for an encore. The lyrics, which smack of ambivalence and angst, are also spot-on for Generation X: "In spite of all the things I do / I still have nothing to say to you." "Succulent" is the outlier of the bunch: a six-minute song where half the running time is devoted to Sonic Youth–style noise. If any potential A&R person liked the first two tracks, it's easy to imagine them being turned off by this one. It was ballsy of the band to record it as part of their demo.

On one of the days Jesse drove Hell back to his apartment after a day of recording, Hell declared that the experience was making him want to play music again. It seems that, after years of musical inactivity, Hell wanted to get the band back together. Not only that, but he wanted Jesse to be a part of it. "It was like the heavens opening up for me," he recalls. Not only was Jesse, at a mere twenty years old, inspiring one of his idols to return to music, but for that idol to then ask him to be part of it was crazy (and more than he could have hoped for). It not only meant the end of college for the foreseeable future but also the end of Worrying Thing. As Jesse says, "I was going to be a Voidoid now."

While Jesse took time off from school to work with Richard Hell, Luke got busy with the newly recorded demo tape, sending out as many copies as was humanly possible. "It was an absolute blitzkrieg," he recalls. He'd been doing this for years. As soon as he got any of his bands on tape or record—going back to when he was in high school—he sent out copies to labels. SST, Dischord, Homestead, City Slang. "You name it," he says. "Every indie label." But he didn't stop there. He'd hit up major operations like CBS, Geffen, and Warner Bros. Not content to just bombard the address or PO box of a record company, he also kept his ears open for potential contacts who worked there. "As soon as I would find out that somebody knew somebody at a label," he explains, "or somebody's cousin had a friend who fixed the plumbing of someone who was at a label, I would start sending them demos." When he later went into the record business, he ran into several people who remembered receiving one of his cassettes. And even if all he got in return was a mountain of rejections, that did nothing to dampen his spirits. "I loved getting the letters," he says. They made him feel that he had some kind of connection to these companies. "I remember in particular getting one from Warner Bros. passing, but I remember feeling deeply moved." The letter had the Warner Bros. logo. "It was like a whisper from God. 'You came to heaven. You can't come in yet. But we acknowledge you exist.'" He was getting closer.

As much as he wanted to get signed and follow his rock star dreams, Luke was also committed to finishing college and getting his degree. Not only that, but his plan was to get a PhD in cultural studies and then become a professor. As an undergrad he was an American studies major, studying areas such as critical theory and third-wave feminism. He began to think about things through the lens of Hegel, Marx, Foucault, and Sartre. This made him want to dissect the idea of capital and its effect on creative output. The best way to do this, Luke figured, was to see what life was like inside one of those record labels he'd so relentlessly pursued. So, as a junior, he got an internship at A&M Records.

He was assigned to the A&R department (A&R stands for "artists and repertoire"; these are the people who sign and work with the talent). The day Luke arrived, he was taken to a room with a box of cassettes and told to return the cassettes with a letter telling whoever had sent the demo that the label was passing. It was painful for him to stuff those envelopes and send back the tapes; he knew what it felt like to get one of those rejection letters, to be on the receiving end of that padded envelope of doom. Even worse, he was shocked to realize that the label wasn't even *listening* to these tapes. To take his mind off this boring and depressing task, he looked around the desks of the A&R reps. He didn't see any traces of the music he was listening to, the independent bands who were out there in the world, waiting to receive a bigger audience. After just three hours, he went to HR and asked to be reassigned. There was one more internship available, in the publicity department. "What's publicity?" he asked. After they explained the job, he said he'd give it a go.

Luke was assigned to Wayne Isaak, who was the general manager of the New York office as well as head of publicity. Big bands on the label were the Police, Joe Jackson, Janet Jackson, Bryan Adams, and Simple Minds. None of those performers meant much to Luke. Then he came across Soundgarden, who'd just signed to A&M. Luke knew the group from their time on indies like SST and Sub Pop. He wondered how an indie group was going to survive at a major label. As Luke got to work doing tour press, he figured that the more he put into the job, the more he'd learn. So he began working eighty hours a week (for free). It wasn't all a success. One night, he worked a party to celebrate Janet Jackson's *Rhythm Nation* and inadvertently turned away star producer Babyface. This landed him in hot water. Luke's response was "Why would I know who Babyface is?" He'd rather have been at a Rites of Spring show.

One day, when his boss was out of the office for lunch, Luke noticed his pay slip sitting on his desk. Luke opened the envelope and looked at the check. He couldn't believe what he saw. *Holy shit,* he thought, *he makes twice what my dad makes, and my dad's a lawyer!* It was the first time Luke realized he might be able to make a living in the world that he'd loved for years.

The internship provided him with another important revelation. "I started to realize there was a burgeoning scene of talent that doesn't really have a culturally connected voice." The labels were signing groups that were big with the college crowd, but they didn't know how to market them.

SAMMY

Having grown up in the scene, Luke figured he could be the connective tissue between indie groups and the world of capital that the major labels represented. He bought a box of fancy stationery, printed out a hundred résumés, and sat down with a spiral-bound directory he'd found at A&M called *The Album Network's Yellow Pages of Rock*. The directory was separated into sections such as Urban Radio, College Radio, Music Retail, and Distribution. It was the industry bible, filled with contact info for everyone in the business. Luke sent out all hundred résumés to people in Los Angeles, asking for a summer job. He got one response. Bryn Bridenthal, who ran Geffen Publicity, called Luke and told him they had an open temp position in the LA office he could interview for. The caveat was that her department was only able to fund the position on a week-to-week basis, so the job could disappear at pretty much any moment. Undaunted, Luke flew out to California and stayed in Bel Air with the mom of a girl he'd been involved with (the relationship hadn't worked out, but the mom still liked him).

Bridenthal got her start as a journalist as well as working in radio in San Francisco before moving south to work at Elektra/Asylum in 1977. When the company moved to New York, she stayed in Los Angeles and opened her own PR firm, working with clients like Mötley Crüe and Queen. She closed the company in 1986 and, after a brief stint at Capitol, joined Geffen Records in 1987. Big acts on the label were Aerosmith, Don Henley, and Guns N' Roses. In the days before voicemail, Luke spent all day, every day wearing a headset and talking to journalists who wanted to set up interviews with Geffen bands. Wanting to make a difference, he looked for the smaller groups he knew he could help—bands like Danzig and Nitzer Ebb, who were more or less orphaned, lost in the huge corporate machinery. The first big score he made was getting a major story placed for Nitzer Ebb while they were opening for Depeche Mode. He discovered from talking with journalists that they were educated and passionate about the music. And they discovered that Luke wasn't just shilling Geffen groups. He could also talk intelligently about Pere Ubu, Neu!, or Suicide. This was a breath of fresh air; they felt like they had one of their own on the other end of the line. He'd end up working at Geffen the entire summer.

When he got back to school, Luke found he couldn't quite leave the music business behind. From his time at A&M and Geffen, he'd seen that there was a need for independent bands to have someone handle their press. To fill this gap, he started his own company. He was soon working with bands like Surgery, Helmet, and Swans. He figured, "I can offer this to them as an indie and do it for them from college." Luke even scored doing PR for that year's New Music Seminar.

As successful as he was doing his own thing, the corporate world soon came calling. Over the holidays, he went to New York to work again with Geffen's Bryn Bridenthal, helping with press for a winter Guns N' Roses tour. He worked through his entire holiday break. In March, Bridenthal reached out yet again. She told Luke she didn't have the budget to hire him as a Geffen employee, but she pledged to hire his PR firm as an independent company, working out of the New York office. He could start the day after graduation. Luke accepted the offer. Graduate school was going to have to wait.

SAMMY

●

After Jesse left Wesleyan in the middle of his junior year, he moved to Manhattan and got an apartment on Fourteenth Street between Avenues B and C. Richard Hell had been approached by a Japanese promoter for a tour the following spring. Hell agreed and decided that Jesse would handle original guitarist Robert Quine's parts, while the other guitarist would be original Voidoid member Ivan Julian. Julian was twenty-two when he first joined, touring with UK soul group the Foundations; in a flash he went from playing "Build Me Up Buttercup" to "Blank Generation." He'd kept busy during the intervening years, playing with his own groups the Outsets and the Lovelies, in addition to taking on session work. As for the bass player and drummer, Jesse was tasked by Hell to find a young and cool rhythm section. "That's when I brought in everybody I knew." For the drummer spot, Jesse's old friend from Great Neck, Michael Corn, auditioned, as did current Worrying Thing member Tim Orr. Orr ended up auditioning three times. "I don't know why Richard was so picky," says Jesse. In the end, Hell turned to Ivan Julian and had him cast around for players. Ivan brought in studio musicians he knew. On bass and keyboards, he drafted a woman named Sue who had experience playing in the orchestra pit of Broadway shows. The job of drummer went to Chuck Clearwater, an eighties heavy metal type who wouldn't have looked out of place in Guns N' Roses (he sported huge blond hair, leather pants, and studded bracelets and belt). Sue and Chuck were able musicians, but it wasn't quite the Replacements-vibe Jesse had been aiming for.

The tour kicked off with a warm-up show at Bard

College that Jesse had booked through his connections to the school. Even though this was Hell's first show in ten years, the students knew him and showered him with love. But the night was not without its drama. Just before hitting the stage, Ivan Julian emerged from his dressing room wearing a fluorescent tank top and spandex pants; he looked more Prince than punk. Hell was taken aback. "What in the fuck are you doing?" Richard roared at the guitarist. Julian stood his ground and the two of them went back and forth trading barbs.

Jesse enjoyed playing with Julian, although their styles were very different. Ivan played lots of flashy solos, seeming to have traded his restrained seventies style for a more glam, over-the-top vibe. Jesse, meanwhile, was finding it hard to fill the shoes of legendary player Robert Quine. Ohio-born Quine was a versatile and innovative player who, after his time in the Voidoids, brought Lou Reed out of a mid-career slump through his work on LPs like *The Blue Mask*. It's not clear to Jesse why Quine wasn't asked back along with Julian. It also didn't take long for Jesse to have a musical awakening. "This whole experience was sort of the moment for me where I realized I'm not a lead guitarist. That's not what I do." When the tour got to Japan, Jesse began to feel the pressure. The first show, in Tokyo, was going to be filmed and professionally recorded in front of a crowd of four thousand people. This was a big deal, and everyone knew it. The band arrived a few days early for a series of rehearsals. Hell was on Jesse's case to improve, telling him, "You're not cutting it." During those first few days in Tokyo, when the rest of the group was out partying and seeing the sites, Jesse was in his hotel room, practicing. "It really felt like I was in trouble," he says. Jesse was more involved, and successful, as a musical director. He came up with an arrangement for a cover of Dylan's "I'll Keep It with Mine" that the band adopted and played.

After the first show went well, the band, the crew, and the promoters celebrated at a fancy and crowded restaurant. There were long tables, and everyone sat on the floor with their shoes off. Hell's entourage numbered around thirty people. Halfway through the meal, a famous Japanese metal band showed up—five guys with matching pink hair and leather jackets, with a dozen girls trailing behind them. They sat twenty feet away from the Hell camp. Everybody associated with the Voidoids was bemused by the entourage except for drummer Chuck Clearwater, who began acting as if he'd finally found his tribe. He kept glancing over at the table, so much so that Jesse said, "Chuck, why don't you just go dive in over there?" Hell, who overheard the remark, told Clearwater he'd pay him a hundred dollars to literally dive, chest first, onto the table of the other party. After replying, "American dollars?" Chuck stood up, ran toward the other group, and dove headfirst onto the table. He slid through thirty feet of glasses, food, and dishes. "It was the loudest crash you'd ever heard," recalls Jesse. "It was mayhem." The Japanese band stood up, angling for a fight. Everyone at the Voidoids table was shell-shocked. A girl sitting at the table with the other band had cut her lip on some of the broken glass and was bleeding. This was when Hell shouted "Run!" and everyone grabbed their shoes and headed for the exit, scampering through the streets of Tokyo in their socks and laughing maniacally. (The incident later became the unreleased Sammy song "Journey to the Center of Japan." Jesse has recently resurrected the track as a Laptop tune called "Indie Hero.")

Upon his return from Japan, Jesse made a big decision. "I was fucking done," he says. Jesse's attitude about the tour was *I did that; I don't need to do that anymore.* It was the ultimate experience; how could he ever top it? He sold his guitar and amp and began to focus more on film. Music—for now—was over.

To make ends meet, he got a job working behind the counter at Rafik Video, a film supply store and editing facility. Around this same time, Sonic Youth was working on promo clips for "Kool Thing" and "Dirty Boots" from their LP *Goo*, the band's first release on major label Geffen. Jesse already knew Thurston Moore a bit since he came into Two Boots. One day, Jesse mentioned that he'd been playing in Richard Hell's band. Thurston didn't know Hell, and Jesse offered to introduce them. "I wanted to bridge the punk rock crowd with the new music crowd," he says. "I felt like that needed to happen." Thurston loved the idea, so Jesse brought Hell to a studio where Sonic Youth was recording. Thurston, Kim Gordon, and Steve Shelley from Sonic Youth were there, as was Minutemen bassist Mike Watt. The introduction ultimately led to Dim Stars, a sort of punk and noise rock supergroup made up of Hell, Shelley, Moore, and Gumball's Don Fleming. Dim Stars recorded and released one self-titled record. Original Voidoid guitarist Robert Quine, who hadn't been asked to play Hell's Japanese tour, was brought back to play on the LP. In a four-star review, *Rolling Stone* called the Dim Stars project "a major contemporary rock event."

Someone else Jesse met at Rafik was director Kelly Reichardt (who, like Thurston Moore, is from Florida; they were born in the same hospital). Jesse and Kelly began dating and collaborating on projects. The first thing they

SAMMY

did together was codirect a video for the song "Bad Mood" by Helmet. Jesse had gotten to know Helmet singer and guitarist Page Hamilton through Phil Hartman's new restaurant the Levee, which Hamilton worked at. While filming the video, Jesse talked Kelly into writing a movie set in Florida, a place she was not looking forward to returning to. "To me it was like, Anywhere but there!" she told *Bomb* magazine in 1995. "It took me 19 years to get out of Miami; I didn't want to go back." Jesse and Kelly traveled to Florida a few times together to do research for her debut film that was released in 1994 as *River of Grass*. Jesse had also made his own short film, *Happy Hour*, which he later ended up taking to several film festivals (it was named Best Short Film at the 1993 Berlin Film Festival). While he was doing all this traveling, he'd listen to mixtapes of new music that Luke had made for him. Jesse, who hadn't been much of a music consumer since leaving college, enjoyed hearing these new bands and songs.

Meanwhile, not only was Luke firmly ensconced in his job at Geffen, but he'd begun performing again. In his first year at the company, needing extra help, he hired Girls Against Boys drummer Alexis Fleisig as a temp. Luke had gotten to know the band's bassist, Johnny Temple, years earlier when they both attended Wesleyan (Temple was a few years ahead). Girls Against Boys, also known as GVSB, was slowly coalescing out of the remains of Soulside, a post-hardcore band from DC that had released two albums on Dischord. Luke was asked to play with GVSB because band member Eli Janney still lived in DC, and they needed someone to cover Janney's parts for local shows. Luke even used his connections to get the band its first show, at Maxwell's out in Hoboken. He also recorded with the group, playing on their first LP, *Tropic of Scorpio*. Playing with GVSB provided Luke with an important realization. "The greatest lesson I've ever learned in rock and roll was probably the first day of rehearsal with Girls Against Boys," he recalls. "Because I remember walking into the room and just hearing the sound of the rhythm section. Scott [McCloud], the guitar player, wasn't even plugged in yet. It was just Johnny and Alexis, and it was the best-sounding fucking band I'd ever been in. And it was just them. And I realized, *Oh, shit, it's the musicians.*" For the remainder of the time he worked with bands, if he didn't get that same instant goose bumps hairs-on-the-back-of-your-neck-stand-up feeling, he wouldn't work with them. More importantly, the experience gave him the itch to once again make music of his own.

Jesse, who ultimately returned to Wesleyan to finish his degree, by now had moved to New York and was living in Manhattan. With Worrying Thing, the song "In Filth" showed there was an idea that hadn't been fully explored: Jesse on vocals and Luke playing lead guitar. Now living in the same city, the pair decided to push the experiment even further, swapping their previous musical roles permanently. But that wasn't all. They both knew they didn't want to stick with the same heavy grunge sound they'd mined while at college. Instead, Jesse and Luke wanted to go back to their roots, taking inspiration from their downtown heroes like the Velvet Underground and Television.

Sammy was about to be born.

2: WHATEVER HAPPENED TO YOU IN THAT CLUB?
Forming, recording, touring, breaking up

By 1992, the American music scene had undergone a seismic shift. *Nevermind*, Nirvana's first major-label album (and only their second overall) hit no. 1 that January, unseating Michael Jackson for the top spot. This ushered in an alternative rock gold rush that lasted most of the decade, with record companies everywhere looking for the next Nirvana. "It felt like every band that had a detuned offset Fender guitar was just going to be explosive," remembers Luke. Seeing as how he'd gone to work for Geffen in May of 1991, just a few months before *Nevermind* came out, Luke found himself at the epicenter of the scene.

That fall, he began working as Sonic Youth's publicist. This was around the time when Sonic Youth and Nirvana were touring together, just before *Nevermind* burst into the stratosphere (the period captured in Dave Markey's documentary *1991: The Year Punk Broke*). Luke spent lots of time with both bands. He also got assigned to be the publicist for Scottish group Teenage Fanclub, whose own second record and major-label debut *Bandwagonesque* came out in November (Spin later named the LP "Record of the Year," a somewhat controversial choice considering how heralded the Nirvana disc was).

It wasn't just that noisy indie bands on major labels were beginning to break through. The college rock scene from the eighties that had given birth to groups like R.E.M., the Replacements, and Hüsker Dü, had transformed into something new: indie rock. Tiny labels like Matador, Merge, Dischord, Teen-Beat, and K were all putting out a wide array of seven-inches and LPs by a huge variety of bands, all of whom bubbled under the surface of the mainstream scene (some buried deeper than others). Luke got a taste of this in late October of 1991 when he attended a benefit for New Jersey radio station WFMU that was headlined by Sonic Youth. (Also on the bill was Dim Stars, the punk-noise supergroup with Richard Hell that Jesse had made possible, and Love Child, a group featuring Rebecca Odes on bass and vocals; she would soon play a part in the Sammy story.) Right before Sonic Youth took the stage, the PA blasted Pavement's "Summer Babe," a song that had been issued as a single by Drag City over the summer. "Immediately I loved it," says Luke. "I was like, *What the fuck is this? This is great!*" Luke's new band would get compared more than once to the idiosyncratic California group. But that was still a few years away.

Jesse was blissfully unaware of most of these events, preferring to think of himself as a filmmaker. However, old habits proved hard to break. During that last year at school, when he'd been living off campus, he found himself writing a new batch of songs. "I got like a Tom Waits–level crap apartment on the bad side of town, above a diner." Going back to get his degree was mainly to please his parents. "When I left school, when I took that break, my mother cried," he recalls. "When I went to Florida to work on the screenplay, she also cried." Jesse peopled his new tunes with characters he'd met at Two Boots or down in Miami: waitresses, teenagers, bartenders, dishwashers. These were the first Sammy songs. After graduation, he moved back to New York.

For Luke, it was a weird and contradictory period. On the one hand, through his job with Geffen, he was surrounded by music every second of every day. When he wasn't listening to music at the office or at home, he was in clubs watching bands perform. Not only that, but he was hobnobbing with all the scene's major players; he often ran into Matador head honcho Gerard Cosloy, and he found himself dropping stuff off at Thurston Moore and Kim Gordon's apartment twice a week. "I was so in the middle of Lower East Side indie rock culture," Luke says. But he wasn't making any music of his own. In fact, the more he witnessed the feeding frenzy of a post-Nirvana world and saw what a hostile space the major-label environment was for independent bands, he wasn't looking to join in anytime soon. "It was such a mess," he says. "And by the way, every artist knew it was a mess. I didn't want to jump into that. But I loved music."

Another development that slowly drew Luke back into the scene was the acquisition of some new gear. He bought a 1959 Fender Jazzmaster from Jerry DiRienzo, guitarist in the band Cell. DiRienzo had himself gotten the instrument from Thurston Moore (Cell was on Moore's boutique label, Ecstatic Peace, which Geffen had begun to distribute). Luke had wanted a whammy bar ever since he heard Dinosaur Jr.'s 1987 LP *You're Living All Over Me*. When he later got a copy of My Bloody Valentine's seminal shoegaze classic *Loveless*, Luke *really* wanted a whammy bar. Long gone was his fascination with the jangly Rickenbacker R.E.M./Paisley

Underground sound. Around when he got the Jazzmaster, Teenage Fanclub gave him a 1963 Fender Princeton amp. They'd been using it on tour but didn't want to ship it back to Scotland. "Thank you for all your work," they said. "Here's an amp." Now that he had all this cool stuff, Luke was thinking to himself, *What do I do with it?*

When he initially reached out to Jesse, now that they were both back in New York, it was to hang out more than anything else. Luke didn't drink, and he was in a long-term relationship with a girl he'd met at college (and would eventually marry), so he and Jesse were not going to go barhopping or prowl the streets looking for dates. Playing guitar at Luke's apartment, and making music, was just an excuse to spend time together. "We had zero ambition to do anything," says Luke. It was just two old college friends hanging out. However, Jesse quickly noticed that something had changed. "Luke had become a really good guitar player." This gave him an idea. "I saw the opportunity to finally say, 'Maybe I should write the lyrics and sing.' It was a kind of *Freaky Friday* moment that worked out." It was perfect timing since Jesse was burnt out on being a lead guitarist after his tour with Richard Hell, whereas Luke had found that spark through his tenure with GVSB and his new gear. In no time they settled into a new paradigm and way of working: Jesse would create the characters and tell the stories, and Luke would shape the sound.

As the pair began to work in earnest on the songs that would make up their first record, they quickly established a way of collaborating that would provide them with material for the life of the band. Jesse would write lyrics to music, something he had either come up with on his own—a riff or chord sequence—or something he'd hammered out with Luke. Jesse wrote music mostly on guitar, although this was a necessity since the only piano he had access to was back at the family home in Great Neck. And while Luke had become proficient with a cassette four-track back in high school, Jesse was never one to create elaborate demos. He'd record just enough to get the song down, sometimes using just a handheld tape recorder. When it came to coming up with the words to go with that music, it was sometimes a struggle. "I wasn't writing poems and then figuring out how to put them to music," he says. Jesse did however keep notebooks in which he scrawled all kinds of ideas: bits of songs, snatches of dialogue, concepts for films. These inspirations covered page after page. To kick-start lyrics, he'd often use a rhyming dictionary. Once he'd written a line that he liked, he'd use the rhyming dictionary to help come up with a direction or sound for the next line. Most often his songs were astutely drawn character studies, tales of losers or small-time gamblers. Rendered in tidy verses and choruses that rhymed, these sketches and portraits went against the prevailing trend in the nineties to offer up nonsense lyrics that didn't mean anything beyond the surface sound of the words themselves. And whereas Jesse wrote the lyrics to Sammy songs, Luke often came up with the titles. Jesse would have been content to name a track after a lyric or phrase in the chorus, but Luke liked offering something more evocative ("Hi-Fi Killers," "Chilling Excerpts," "Leopard Skin Swatch"). Today, Jesse calls these choices "the Luke layer on top of my lyrics."

Much of the music Jesse was writing lyrics to had been hammered out with Luke at his West Village apartment at

SAMMY

123 Bank Street. Situated just a block from the Hudson River on a charming tree-lined cobblestone street, the two would sit with their guitars on a pair of Eero Saarinen stools Luke had borrowed from the family home upstate. "There was an incredibly small and hot underground room in this bizarrely configured studio duplex," Luke recalls. "It had no windows, was next to the building furnace, and had my bed." It also had a 1976 silver-face Twin Reverb, which Luke would plug his Jazzmaster into. Seeing as how Jesse had shed all his gear after his tour as a Voidoid, for these initial sessions he borrowed Luke's G&L ASAT, which was basically a Telecaster. Luke, heavily influenced by Sonic Youth, employed several alternate tunings, mainly in open D such as DADAGD, DADABE, and DDAFAD. Since he considered Jesse to be the superior player, Luke opted for odd, angular, or unexpected bits of accompaniment. These parts, inspired by Robert Quine, added a lot to Sammy's overall sound and ensured that they didn't sound like every other Seattle grunge clone that came along in the wake of Nirvana.

As the songs began to multiply, and the idea of starting a new band—rather than just hanging out—began to solidify, Jesse figured he needed a guitar of his own. Around this same time, a friend of his, Joel Schlemowitz, was making a feature film of Leopold von Sacher-Masoch's novella *Venus in Furs* (the book that provided the inspiration for the Velvet Underground song). Jesse was playing Severin. There was no room in the budget to pay anyone, but after working on the film for a bit, Jesse discovered the filmmaker had in his closet a 1966 Fender Jaguar. The filmmaker gave Jesse the guitar as payment for being in the film. Now that both Jesse and Luke had their chosen instruments, and they had a batch of new tunes, they had a decision to make: What should they call themselves?

Sammy takes shape: Jesse on his Jaguar and Luke on his Jazzmaster. Courtesy of Jesse Hartman.

After batting around a few other choices, none of which either Jesse or Luke can remember, they settled on Sammy. It's based on Jesse's middle name, Samuel, the name of his paternal grandfather. An added inspiration was the diner Sammy's Roumanian on the Lower East Side. "The old Jewish-name vibe of it was kind of appealing," says Jesse. "It had a schmaltzy, Vegas-y feel to it. In retrospect, it's not such a good name with the internet and Google searches." (I can attest to that last part; looking online for "Sammy music" turns up a lot of results for Sammy Hagar and Sammy Davis Jr.) Reflecting on the name now, Luke laughs and says, "We were self-abashedly dooming our career from the start."

Another key choice they made early on, and one that consciously or unconsciously helped determine the group's fate, was the decision to not invite anyone else into the band. "We never needed a drummer," says Luke. "It was a sonic necessity, but we never actually wanted or thought about having someone else in Sammy." They figured either one of them could play bass parts, and drummers would be drafted in and out as needed for recording sessions or shows. It seemed to work for the Fastbacks.

After the duo had captured several crude demos at Luke's apartment throughout the fall of 1992, they decided they were ready to move to the next step: recording. Luke had recently spent time at Manhattan's Magic Shop with producer du jour Butch Vig as Sonic Youth was finishing up their second Geffen LP, *Dirty*. Luke had also been listening to Steve Albini's mixes from Nirvana's *In Utero* sessions as they were delivered to the Geffen offices. Luke's feeling was *We can't do that*. It didn't feel right to take Sammy into a twenty-four-track studio at $500 a day. The burgeoning lo-fi movement, spearheaded by groups like Sebadoh, the Mountain Goats, Guided by Voices, and the Magnetic Fields, showed there was another way: You could record at home. "There was a whole world of stuff that was smaller-sounding," Luke says. "And it felt like a great answer to the enormity of *Siamese Dream*, *Nevermind*, and *Loveless*."

Even though Luke was the one with all the industry and band contacts, it was Jesse who came up with the answer. He thought back to Great Neck, to his friend Michael Corn's basement, where they'd made those elaborate home recordings of his high school band the Sy's. Jesse knew that Corn had stayed close to Great Neck after high school and was still living at home. Even though he got into both Purchase College and SUNY Oneonta, Corn opted to attend nearby Queens College so he could continue to live in Great Neck. This gave him the opportunity to further hone his musical and recording chops. For Sammy to head to Corn's house seemed like the ideal solution since Corn was not only a good engineer but also a great drummer. In the years since the Sy's, Corn had upgraded from a cassette four-track to an eight-track. As Luke recalls, "The stakes were wildly low." They just wanted to record *something*.

Double exposure shot with Michael Corn, Jesse, and Luke recording the Sammy demo. Courtesy of Michael Corn.

In late January of 1993, Jesse and Luke headed out to Long Island, set up their gear in Corn's basement, and bashed out four songs: "Babe Come Down," "Evergladed," "Death Motel" and "Roach Girl." They did two takes of each song except for "Roach Girl," which they only played once. At the time "Evergladed," which had gone by the titles "In Filth" and "Filth Glazed" during the Worrying Thing days, was now known by yet another name: "Sea of Grass."

Corn had met Luke prior to this, having hung out with him and Jesse one night in the city. When they first met, Corn couldn't believe how animated and outgoing Luke was without the aid of any form of drug or narcotic. "He seemed to be this sort of naturally high character," Corn

SAMMY

remembers. Luke, who had never heard Corn play, trusted Jesse's recommendation. When they got to Great Neck, Luke discovered that Corn was indeed super musical and technical. And while Corn didn't have an emotional connection to the style of music that Jesse and Luke wanted to play, that turned out to not be a bad thing. Instead, Corn treated the day like a session musician, asking Jesse and Luke, "What do you guys want me to play?"

After quickly mixing down the best takes of the four songs, they went down the block to Jesse's house to give what they'd recorded a listen. It had been a long day, and the plan was for Luke to spend the night in the upstairs guest room. Before they turned in, they played the songs in Jesse's basement. The pair couldn't believe what they heard. "It was surprising how good it was," Jesse says. Their low expectations were one of the reasons why the results came out the way they did. "We were uninhibited," says Luke. "We had no rules, and we didn't care. That makes it easy." They had meant to just be cutting demos, but what they heard in that basement in Long Island at one-thirty in the morning was good enough to be released.

As soon as Luke got back to the office, he began making copies of the Sammy demo, the same as he'd done for Worrying Thing and Nehru Zombie before that. This time, he didn't need to rely on an industry directory or any sort of generic letter that began *To whom it may concern*. Instead, he just gave out cassettes to people he was dealing with every day, contacts like Dan Koretzky from Drag City and Steve Shelley from Sonic Youth (Shelley had started a label called Smells Like Records in 1992). Shelley, who joined Sonic Youth as their second and final drummer in 1985, liked the cassette and offered to put out a single. Seeing as how the first Smells Like release was a seven-inch by Sentridoh, an ultra-lo-fi acoustic side project from Sebadoh's Lou Barlow, Sammy's basement recording was going to fit in perfectly on Smells Like. When asked about perhaps pursuing a bigger indie label like Merge or Matador, Luke answers, "We didn't care. We had no aspirations." They just thought it was cool that Steve Shelley from Sonic Youth wanted to work with them. So why not give it a shot? From the January sessions, they chose "Babe Come Down" and "Roach Girl."

It's fitting that "Babe Come Down" became Sammy's debut single since it was also the first song Jesse and Luke wrote for their new group. More than that, according to Luke, "This was the most important song for me because finally Jesse and I had a 'sound' that I'd always been chasing." They were no longer recycling old material, or merely paying tribute to their heroes. Instead, this was the sound of two friends collaborating and connecting, expressing themselves individually but with absolute unity. "The lead line was the first lead line I ever wrote for Sammy, and it's still my favorite," says Luke. The lyrics were inspired by a waitress at Two Boots named Anna who left to waitress at Three of Cups, a new restaurant around the corner started by Santo Fazio, a longtime Two Boots chef and part-time actor. Jesse was close to Santo, having directed him in the short film he made in college, *Happy Hour*. (He'd later have Santo star in his 2008 film *House of Satisfaction*.)

The guitar bends in B-side "Roach Girl" were inspired by Teenage Fanclub's "Everything Flows," a track on the group's first LP, 1990's *A Catholic Education*. John Steeb, the bass player from Worrying Thing, had turned Luke onto the group at Wesleyan. Luke would later witness dozens of shows during the *Bandwagonesque* tour. "I watched Raymond

[McGinley] play those bends every night and I was like, *Wow, that's really cool.*" Lyrically, Jesse's tale about a girl he knew growing up in Great Neck shows that—even in this early stage of the group—the narrative template was being set. "The song is a short story and gives you a glimpse that Jesse was already creating character worlds with every song," says Luke. "It's an incredibly tender lyric in the chorus about a very tragic character." Jesse likes it too. Discussing it thirty years later, he remarks, "It should have been on the album."

With Luke in manager mode, Jesse slipped back into the film world for a while. *Happy Hour* was beginning to make the rounds of film festivals, and he was gearing up to produce *River of Grass* over the summer, the screenplay he'd cowritten with Kelly Reichardt the previous year. Even though graphic design was not one of Luke's skills, he kickstarted the design for the single. While shopping in a vintage store with Liz Phair, whom he was trying to get to sign to Geffen, he found an old photo of a car as well as a bunch of pictures of dogs. The shot of the car went on the front and the dogs on the back. In New York, Jesse finished the job by xeroxing the Sammy logo over and over to get it to look old and distressed. Michael Corn's drumming was credited to just "Corn." His name would appear in the same form on the first Sammy album when it was released in 1994.

Illustrating just how much Jesse's film and music worlds overlapped around this time, when he was in Berlin in February for a film festival, Luke told him to look up Christof Ellinghaus from the German indie label City Slang. Luke knew Christof and thought maybe he'd like to put out the Sammy seven-inch in Europe. At the end of a long day of festival activities, Jesse met up with Christof somewhere in Berlin. They sat in Ellinghaus's car and Jesse played him the Sammy tape. "Babe Come Down" blasted throughout the small space, and Christof seemed to be digging it. Jesse thought it was going well. And then Christof turned to him and said, "It sounds a little like Pavement." City Slang did not put out the seven-inch.

When Jesse got the finished copies of the Smells Like single, it was June, and he was in Florida making *River of Grass*. Even though it was a small independent film made on a shoestring budget, there was a thirty-person crew, and Jesse, who was acting as producer, spent most of the production in the office dealing with details. Holding the seven-inch in his hand, and marveling at the fact that it was the first time his music had been pressed to vinyl, he felt the pendulum swing back in the other direction. Sammy was calling.

Despite the band's momentum, recording an album was never a foregone conclusion. "Our plan was not to make a full-length," says Luke. "It was just that we had these songs, so let's bring them to life." To do this, in early August, Jesse and Luke once again headed out to Long Island. Michael Corn, who'd drummed and engineered the first batch of Sammy tunes, was now writing jingles for Jack Malken, a producer and musician who'd been in the band Thirty Days Out in the early seventies. Malken worked out of his Great Neck home, a white and angular house that was open and airy. That's where Corn had set up all his gear. Despite it being a more modern and bigger space, the guys preferred the first setup. "The room didn't have a sound; it didn't have a vibe," says Luke. "We actually liked Corn's basement better as a feel." They also think the four tracks they did at Corn's house sound better. Recording at Malken's home bothered Luke for another reason. His concern was that since they weren't paying Malken anything, Luke didn't want him to later claim that he owned the rights to the tapes or the recordings. "I'm the son of a litigator," explains Luke, "so I spend my life not wanting to get sued."

Luke laying down guitar for Debut Album. *Courtesy of Jesse Hartman.*

Even though the sessions were quick and productive (everything was recorded in less than a week), it was a weird period for both Jesse and Luke. Neither of them completely had their heads in the music, nor were they convinced about the idea of Sammy being a conventional band. Jesse was making real strides in the film world, having just produced his first feature film, and Luke was making a name for himself as a high-powered publicist at Geffen. This meant the activity out in Great Neck had to sometimes take a back seat. "When we were recording the record," Corn remembers, "Luke would stop and take breaks and have long conversations with Kurt Cobain."

Just a few weeks after the LP was recorded, Luke moved from New York to Los Angeles. The relocation was prompted by matters professional and personal. Geffen's LA office was the heart of the company's operations, whereas the outpost in Manhattan was essentially a satellite to California's main headquarters. Also, seeing as how Luke's wife was embarking on an MFA in writing at USC, it made perfect sense to move out West. The Geffen offices were on Sunset Boulevard just a few blocks from the Roxy, Viper Room, and Whisky a Go Go (Sammy would later play at the Roxy and Viper Room). Luke's spacious new office housed a multi-component stereo with studio monitor speakers, stacks of CDs, a TV, and several large plants. On the walls he hung posters for Geffen acts such as Sonic Youth, Nirvana, and Teenage Fanclub, not to mention a framed print advertising the first Lollapalooza. The move was big enough industry news that it got reported in *Billboard*: "Luke Wood is relocating to the West Coast office in September to join the marketing department."

Luke, who grew up in snowy, cold Rochester, loved Los Angeles. He rented a house on a hill in Silver Lake not far from the reservoir, ten miles from the office. In the early nineties, Silver Lake was home to a vibrant local scene, with small but vital venues like Spaceland, Jabberjaw, and Raji's playing host to groups such as Touchcandy, Lutefisk, Popdefect, Babyland, and dozens of others (including my own rock combo, Bespin Fatigues). This fertile environment would soon produce Beck, whose smash hit "Loser" was recorded in a Los Angeles living room. Luke quickly made use of his new space, setting up a small studio in the basement. After spending years in studios with A&R people whom he felt were clueless about the actual ins and outs of recording, Luke made it his mission to learn how to engineer and make music. And after suffering in the cramped confines of his duplex in Greenwich Village, he was now able to get some serious gear. This would soon come in handy for Sammy.

With the tracks for their first LP recorded, the next step was designing the cover. Label boss Steve Shelley let Jesse and Luke handle the design. Jesse asked his friend Larry Fessenden for help. A native New Yorker as well as a ridiculously prolific actor, screenwriter, director, editor, and songwriter, Fessenden has made or starred in dozens of independent and mainstream features and TV shows (including Jesse's college short *Happy Hour*, and the Hartman-produced *River of Grass*). His work was even the subject of a 2022 retrospective at Manhattan's Museum of Modern Art entitled "Oh, the Humanity!" (*River of Grass* was shown, as was Fessenden's 1995 film *Habit*, which features Jesse in a role as well as a Sammy song on the soundtrack.) Much of Fessenden's work centers around the horror genre, and is made via his long-standing independent production company, Glass Eye Pix, which has been operating out of New York for more than forty years. Jesse and Larry met in the early nineties through Fessenden's hanging around Two Boots.

In terms of why he was chosen to help with the artwork, Fessenden says, "I was the guy with the computer and skills in QuarkXPress." He was also designing posters, flyers for gigs, and more. The cover that Jesse and Fessenden came up with for *Debut Album* was a vintage shot of a pu pu platter (a plate of appetizers usually made of Hawaiian or Chinese food). The group's name, and the name of the album, is laid out in lowercase letters of blue (the band name) and red (the album name) against bands of white on the top and bottom. On the back is a picture of Jesse at age seven taken on July

4, 1976, at a bicentennial party in Great Neck (pictured on page 26). The interior has a similar snapshot of Luke as a kid. The liner notes are handwritten. The overall package feels very indie rock.

Drummer and engineer Michael Corn is listed again simply as "Corn," a credit which would cause not only confusion (some reviews called him "the mystery drummer") but also conspiracy theories. One rumor began to circulate that, because Sammy was on Steve Shelley's label, "Corn" was simply an alias for the Sonic Youth drummer. This was of course not true, but Shelley did drum with the group on at least one occasion. In addition to album credits, the liner notes also list the addresses for both Jesse's East Village apartment and Luke's new Los Angeles home, thus relaying to listeners that this was a bicoastal band. Luke also includes an email address, something which was cutting-edge in 1994.

Before *Debut Album* came out, Jesse and Luke did a photo shoot with Spike Jonze in front of Sammy's Roumanian in NYC; Luke and Spike were friends. Another thing that Luke handled prior to the record's release was to negotiate a deal for the album to be issued in the UK on Fire Records. Seeing as how Sammy didn't have proper management, and Luke was busy with work stuff at the time, this took around four months.

Fire was a small independent UK label started in 1985 by Johnny Waller and Clive Solomon. In its early years, Fire had released a variety of interesting records, including the first couple of Pulp albums. Before Nirvana hit it big, Fire was handling mostly reissues (including the Spacemen 3 record Luke had loved so much in high school). In the early nineties, John Wells, a lawyer based in New York (and a friend of Luke's), got in touch with Clive Solomon and offered to be the liaison between Fire and small American labels like K and Smells Like. The plan was for Wells to funnel to Fire stuff that wasn't already getting licensed elsewhere. This would show the British music press that Fire was a hip label, and this would in turn lead to bigger signings. K groups Fitz of Depression and Halo Benders would end up signing to Fire in addition to Sammy.

While Luke's move to the West Coast at the end of the summer was a big event in his life, a change in Jesse's came closer to the end of the year. For a few years, Two Boots had hosted parties on New Year's Eve where bands would play. One of the acts playing Two Boots on New Year's Eve in 1993 was Love Child. (On this same night, Luke was at the Metro in Chicago at a Liz Phair show, still trying to woo her to Geffen. Veruca Salt was the opening act. "The second I saw Veruca Salt," Luke remembers, "I was like, *Oh, sign that band too*.") Love Child, which initially included Alan Licht on guitar and vocals, Rebecca Odes on bass and vocals, and Will Baum on drums, formed in 1987 when all three were students at Vassar College in upstate New York. The group lasted roughly five years, releasing two LPs on Homestead (1991's *Okay?* and 1992's *Witchcraft*) and a clutch of singles on independent labels. Their first album featured short tracks that were often noisy and catchy at the same time; the single "Sofa" mixes sing-song repetition of the cozy phrase "I wanna sit with you on the sofa" with bursts of white noise. By their second LP, which saw drummer Brendan O'Malley join the lineup, the songs became longer and more accomplished. "AAA/XXX," which is sung by Rebecca Odes, is about having lustful thoughts while waiting for a mechanic. It's clever, sexy, and a lot of fun. Love Child played with several well-known indie groups, such as Yo La Tengo, Galaxie 500, Pavement, and Sonic Youth. They also toured Europe with Sub Pop's Codeine. Major labels came sniffing around after *Witchcraft* dropped, but nothing came of it and the group soon disbanded.

Jesse and Rebecca Odes onstage with Sammy at Two Boots.
Courtesy of Jesse Hartman.

That New Year's Eve at Two Boots, Jesse and Rebecca met. Jesse was tending bar. "As I remember it," she says, "I went up for a drink on my way out, and we sort of locked in. I had come with a crew from Hoboken who were all mad at me for lingering." Rebecca already knew about Jesse because friends from the scene had mentioned him, plus their paths had almost crossed at a practice space used by Yo La Tengo and a bunch of other bands. "People kept talking about this

SAMMY

guy Jesse," Rebecca remembers. "I was intrigued that there was someone around I didn't already know, who had been coexisting in some parallel orbit—so I was kind of primed to be figuring out what he was about." They very quickly became a couple. She would go on to play several shows with Sammy, including accompanying Jesse and Luke—and Love Child drummer Brendan O'Malley—on a pivotal trip overseas in November. It's easy to see why Jesse and Rebecca got together: both are smart, musical, and local (Odes grew up in West Orange, New Jersey), and both loved the Velvet Underground. It was magic. Or, as Jesse would put it in a song he'd write and record the following year about the night they met, "Majik."

The year 1994 was big for indie rock, seeing the release of *Bee Thousand*, Guided by Voices' best album, Pavement's career highlight *Crooked Rain, Crooked Rain*, as well as strong records by Dinosaur Jr., Sebadoh, and many others. This year also marked an end of an era. When Kurt Cobain's body was found on the morning of April 8, it signaled the beginning of the end of grunge and the alternative scene in general. Despite the success of big records such as *Ill Communication* by Beastie Boys, Soundgarden's *Superunknown*, and debuts by Weezer and Beck, the demise of Nirvana not only took the wind out of the sails of alternative rock, it pretty much capsized the boat. Britpop soon filled the gap, with young and hungry groups like Oasis more than willing to accept the attention and crowds that came with massive success (hell, Oasis was writing about the drug-fueled life of a "Rock 'n' Roll Star" before they were stars). This was the world in which Sammy released *Debut Album*.

The record kicks off with "Rudy." Luke and Jesse had worked out the music together, and Jesse then took home a tape and wrote the lyrics. The words were inspired by characters he saw hanging around, or working at, his brother's East Village pizza place. Rudy was a Rastafarian dishwasher at Two Boots who was in his late twenties. Jesse, who had worked there for years, spent a lot of time with him. "When you have to stay until two in the morning with the dishwasher, you're going to hang out and you're going to talk." The lack of digital devices also meant people had no choice but to connect. "There were no phones," Jesse adds. "There were no laptops. There was nothing to distract you. You had to kind of get to know each other." The song also includes other neighborhood characters, such as a petty gangster named Jerry who ran numbers and kept tabs on his clients with a pad of paper and pen he always carried around ("You were running numbers, and I placed a bet"). Jesse had been writing about these neighborhood fixtures as far back as "The Regular" from his high school band the Sy's. "I grew up as a restaurant kid." Millie's, Great Jones Café, Two Boots. All of them provided Jesse with an endless amount of material. "That is the great thing about a restaurant. You're connecting with people that you really would not necessarily connect with in your regular life." Luke's lead guitar line was played on his Jazzmaster run through a 1984 ProCo RAT plugged into his Twin Reverb.

Next up is "Hi Fi Killers," a fun tune that imagines what it might be like to date a riot grrrl, a musical scene that was in ascendance in the early nineties. Seeing as how Jesse had no idea who groups like Huggy Bear and Bikini Kill were, the concept came from Luke. "I wasn't paying too much attention to our peers," Jesse admits. And while the lyrics, at first glance, read as tongue-in-check—Hartman's narrator telling his feminist girlfriend that maybe she could take a brief break from her political demonstrations so they can spend a little time together ("Take a night off your riot / We could sneak you out quiet")—the song also offers an empathetic view of the frustration young women were feeling ("How'd you get so damn tough? You must have had enough"). Says Luke, "It's about the friction of cultural signifiers and affairs of the heart." You can lose a lover to all kinds of things: a rival, an ex, drug addiction, or—as is chronicled here—a scene (the character lamenting, "Why'd you have to go away?"). Seeing as how this was from the second batch of the initial group of Sammy songs, Jesse and Luke by now were writing to the sound of the band.

Third track "Dim Some" is the record's longest, clocking in at 4:41. "That song is about me walking around New York by myself," says Jesse. "The lonely guy cruising through Chinatown." The title, a pun on the Chinese dish dim sum, speaks to the narrator's longing, with Jesse's mumbling of "dim sum" slowly transforming into "dim some" and finally "gimme some," thus articulating the drive of the narrator to create a connection with anything. The "dancing chickens" Jesse mentions in the track refer to an arcade called Chinatown Fair, which presented live chickens in machines, and for fifty cents, you could either make a chicken dance or challenge it to a game of tic-tac-toe (a sign on the contraption declared LARGE BAG OF FORTUNE COOKIES IF YOU BEAT THE CHICKEN). Luke's not sure if there's bass guitar on the track or if it's just a regular guitar playing the lower riff. "There's way less bass on *Debut Album* than I thought," he marvels. "It definitely speaks to the fact we didn't have a bass player." His extended solo was inspired by two periods of guitarist Robert Quine's work: his playing on the Tom Waits classic "Rain Dogs" as well as Matthew Sweet's "Girlfriend."

Luke describes "Shoot It Around!" as the first "traditional" rock song he and Jesse recorded as Sammy, taking inspiration from hard-hitting tunes ranging from "Gimme Shelter" by the Rolling Stones to Sonic Youth's "Silver Rocket" (with Luke also paying homage to Dinosaur Jr. with all that whammy bar). With this track Jesse also developed a new way of singing. "This was the first song I remember where Jesse had a toughness in the vocal performance," says Luke. "It's like another character he was developing." The subject of the song is ostensibly a guy showing a girl around New York (there are mentions of the tourist cruise the Circle Line and taking a dip in Long Island Sound, a body of water off the coast where Jesse grew up). But the tune's romance goes well beyond mere boy-meets-girl; it's boy-meets-NYC. "When you grow up in Great Neck, but the adventure is forty-five minutes away in the city," says Luke, "you spend a lot of time thinking about how to get there." In the end, however, no matter how proud Jesse's narrator is of his town, or New York City in general, "Shoot It Around!" is another brilliant and effective tale of longing and trying to make a connection, Jesse crooning to his accidental tourist: "I just want to know you better."

"The Turtle" is a strange tune created while they were recording the album, with Luke sitting in on drums. The electronic burbles at the end came from pitch-bending stock sounds on Corn's Yamaha DX7 keyboard. The song's subject is serial killer Joel Rifkin, who was nicknamed "the Turtle" by classmates due to his shuffling walk and constant slouching. These same classmates relentlessly and ruthlessly bullied Rifkin for years. (There's also a season 5 episode of *Seinfeld* where Elaine's boyfriend is named Joel Rifkin.) The song sprang from Jesse's long-standing interest in the seamy underbelly of society, a fascination that was constantly fueled by tabloids the *New York Post* and the *Daily News*, which often featured lurid headlines and stories of murder and mayhem. A later track on *Debut Album* would deal with similar subject matter.

Following debut single "Babe Come Down" is "Fantastic Sam," which sees Jesse introduce yet another theme in his lyrics: giving advice to troubled guy friends he was close to who were grappling with something important or hard in their lives. "I had a few friends who were coming to terms with their sexuality, and a little bit troubled by it all, and sometimes I would play the role of adviser." This song was written about Worrying Thing bassist John Steeb, whom Jesse loved and whose life was beginning to spiral out of control due to drugs. The long outro has nods to *White Light/White Heat* era Velvet Underground, which was fitting given how Jesse and Luke met. As part of that outro, Jesse speak-sings, "I got my own problems." Sure, he's helping his friends, but who's going to help him?

"Rico & Carl" is a harder edged tune that owes a bit to Luke's tenure in Girls Against Boys and his love of Sonic Youth. Seeing as how Sammy was not a traditional band with guitar, drums, and bass, Luke had to often fill in the gaps. "This is probably one of the first songs where I played bass, and Jesse and I started to lock in where the bass part and guitar part are tight and hard to differentiate." This is partly because, seeing as how he hadn't been trained to play the instrument, Luke tended to approach the bass as if it were a guitar. Lyrically, "Rico & Carl" kicks off with the start of a road trip: "Let's take a ride / all the way down I-95." The inspiration was one of Jesse's many trips to Florida. "It was very different in those days," he says. "There was something much more seedy and strange about it. It was quirkier, and I was kind of obsessed with it." The song is named after a couple of guys Jesse met when he was in the Sunshine State working on *River of Grass*.

"Evergladed" comes next on the LP. It's the oldest song Sammy ever recorded, and the only one with roots in an earlier group. It's also, as you can tell from its title, yet another track inspired by Florida. The area is referenced in the opening narration to *River of Grass*: "Most tourists visit the Miami area for its beaches on the East Coast, but if you ever mistakenly get on the Palmetto Expressway and head west, you'd run right into the Florida Everglades." Known for its huge forest of mangroves, the everglades were known to the Native Americans who first lived there as *Pa-hay-Okee*, which means "grassy waters." The chordal voicing in the tune comes from Luke, who took as his inspiration GVSB and Fugazi. There's also a whole bunch of whammy bar. "I can't say enough how the whammy was a big part of my approach to guitar playing," he says. "We wanted everything to be a little woozy—a little floaty." When it came time to make a video for a track off *Debut Album*, Larry Fessenden once again helped, directing a no-budget clip on 8 mm for "Evergladed" (as Jesse says, "It was a big Larry year"). The outdoor shots were filmed in winter in the courtyard behind Two Boots, Jesse sitting on a bucket. "There was snow on the ground, and we played with that," says Fessenden. "I had him lip-sync, and I lit it like a Weegee photo with a 'sun gun' as the light faded." The footage of Jesse, Luke, and Corn performing were shot at the band's rehearsal space,

Context Studios, which was just down the street from Two Boots. This is also where Jesse had rehearsed with Richard Hell and held the Voidoids auditions back in 1990.

Whereas "Rico & Carl" was about a road trip, "Royal Flush" is about trying to pass the hours of a long flight, something Jesse spent a lot of time doing in the early nineties as he flew back and forth from film festivals and trips to research *River of Grass*. In addition to playing poker, the lyrics mention using all those hours to write a letter, before nodding off only to have a nightmare about the plane crashing. Musically, the track came together quickly. As Luke recalls, "We had a ton of fun recording it. It's all assertion and bravado, and then you have this super-simple silly solo that makes you think, *Maybe these guys aren't as hard as they think they are*." The outro is Sammy once again channeling the Stones.

Debut Album starts to wind down with "TZ Queen," yet another tune inspired by Jesse's trips to Florida. While making *River of Grass*, Jesse and the film's director, Kelly Reichardt, stayed with Reichardt's parents. While there, Jesse got to know Kelly's teenage stepsister. "She was in another world," he remembers. Jesse was bemused and fascinated by her inscrutability. "A teenage Zombie queen," he writes in the track, "she's only fourteen." This was also one of the first "full band" songs Jesse and Luke recorded; it contains a bass line and several guitar parts (including a slide guitar bit Luke played with a beer bottle).

Final song is "Room No. 8 (DM 2)." Tracks like this, with Luke laying down leads over Jesse's rhythm guitar, were a complete reversal of the roles in their college band. Having jurisdiction over this new sonic territory invited Luke to expand how he played. Another element that contributed to

Luke's parts was his guitar. "I can't articulate loudly enough how the Jazzmaster just gave me confidence and feel and desire to play all these lines," he says. "For me, Jesse was my copilot, but the Jazzmaster was my engine." The song's subject is once again Jesse's fascination with true crime. In fact, it's sort of a sequel to the earlier B-side "Death Motel" (the parenthetical "DM 2" in the song's title stands for "Death Motel 2"). That track was about a child investigating the death of his father at the hands of a gay hustler (shades of the incident with Jesse's high school science teacher), which "Room No. 8" references in its final seconds, Jesse saying, "He popped your pop."

In the US, "Rudy" quickly got added to shows like KCRW's *Subterranean Soundwaves*, while in the UK *Debut Album* rose as high as no. 4 on the indie LP charts. Meanwhile, reviews were almost uniformly positive. Writing for *Vox*, Ann Scanlon gave the LP a seven out of ten and declared that "*Debut Album* is a classic example of quickly recorded (it was completed in a week) yet highly affecting music." Metal publication *Raw* rated the record four out of five, calling it "Good stuff that causes the knee to jerk spasmodically in time to the healthy, wholesome solid groove."

In *Melody Maker*, Everett True praised *Debut Album* as sounding like "the Sears Tower at midnight, dusty railtracks lying idle in the midday sun, slacker boys in smocks and flannel trying to catch the latest Winona Ryder movie, cut-price Woolworths Sales, clumsy chat-up lines enacted in front of tumbling shopping mall waterfalls . . . the very essence of Americana, in fact." A music journalist who got his start in the eighties, by the early nineties Everett True (a pseudonym; he was born Jeremy Andrew Thackray) became one of the first to chronicle the rising grunge scene. He eventually got so cozy with Kurt Cobain he pushed him onto stage at the 1992 Reading Festival in a wheelchair. He would be much less charitable the next time he wrote about Sammy, but for now, anyway, he was a fan.

Reviewing *Debut Album* for the *NME*, Keith Cameron addressed the elephant in recording studio head-on, writing, "Sammy sound like Pavement. A lot like Pavement." But he then added, "The good news is that none of this matters one jot." He enjoyed the album, giving it eight out of ten and concluding, "Talent borrows, we have been advised, while genius steals. Sammy manage to do both simultaneously. You'll love it." Eric T. Miller, in *Magnet*, hit the same theme, writing, "Yep, Sammy has a Pavement fixation. But that's cool with me 'cause I'm one of those people that believes Stephen Malkmus and bandmates comprise one of the planet's best bands."

The Pavement comparisons would persist over the ensuing years. As *Trouser Press* would later write, "Sammy's first longplayer sounds so much like Pavement that the resemblance hits like a yard of concrete." Jesse had heard this before Sammy's first single even came out, way back in 1993 when he played "Babe Come Down" for City Slang's Christof Ellinghaus. And to this day, more than thirty years later, whenever Sammy is written about online or discussed, Pavement is usually mentioned as well (often pejoratively; words like "copycat" and "rip-off" are sometime used).

I should state at this point, and for the record, that I'm a Pavement fan. I've seen the group live numerous times over the decades, including their first US tour in support of *Slanted and Enchanted*. I was living in Columbia, South

Carolina, and, after their gig at a tiny bar called Rockafellas, I approached Malkmus and asked if I could score a quick interview. He politely demurred, saying they were about to hop in their van to head off for their next show in Georgia. I replied that was no problem, and the following day, I made my way to Atlanta. Once I found the venue, a huge nightclub called Masquerade that boasted three stages, Mark Ibold and Bob Nastanovich were kind enough to give me a half hour of their time. They were each approachable and friendly. I wanted to speak to them because I'd been knocked out by Pavement's debut LP (here's how I described *Slanted and Enchanted* in the introduction to my interview, which was published that October in the zine *Indie File*: "It's a brilliant disc full of hard and soft songs, a lot of ranting and raving, some great drumming, and more hooks than a bait shop"). Later, in 1994, after I'd returned to Los Angeles, I bought the band's second LP, *Crooked Rain, Crooked Rain*, at Aron's Records in Hollywood the day it came out, February 14. To show how big Pavement was during this period, the guy in front of me in line was also buying a copy of *Crooked Rain*. So was the guy behind me. I then proceeded to spend a lonely Valentine's Day night enraptured with the album while also trying to eat my loneliness by consuming an entire Bigfoot pizza from Pizza Hut (don't ask).

So as a fan of both Sammy and Pavement, yes, I hear the similarities. It'd be disingenuous, if not plain dishonest of me, to not acknowledge this. The resemblance is something that even the most casual listener can pick up on (a few months ago when I blasted *Debut Album*, excited after first talking to Jesse and Luke about this book, my wife walked into the living room, pointed to the speakers, and said, plainly, "Pavement?"). I won't be evasive or defensive about this point. It should also be noted that neither is Jesse nor Luke defensive about this. During that first call, when I tried to sell the duo on my vision for this book (and thus cement their participation in it), I felt I had to bring up Pavement. It was a subject I knew I'd have to tackle if I wanted to tell the story of Sammy. Reluctantly, and almost apologetically, I said that, during my interviews, I'd have to ask them about the Sammy-sounds-like-Pavement claim/debate/accusation. To my surprise, Jesse and Luke readily agreed. In fact, they laughed it off. I'd been half-worried the topic might derail our conversation and kill the entire project right there, but as it turned out, they couldn't have cared less.

Despite any sonic comparisons, what can't be denied is how similar Pavement and Sammy are in their DNA. Both bands grew out of the nucleus of two friends who began making music together without much of a strategy to do anything with it. In the case of Pavement, Stephen Malkmus and Scott Kannberg were friends who grew up in Stockton, California. Both Malkmus and Kannberg played guitar, sang, and wrote songs. Early Pavement singles, the first of which they put out themselves in 1989 before signing initially to Drag City before moving to Matador, were lo-fi affairs featuring just Malkmus and Kannberg playing guitar and bass. And like Sammy's relationship with Michael Corn, Pavement enlisted a guy in town, Gary Young, who owned recording equipment and who played drums, to round out their sound and capture their tunes on tape. (Unlike Corn, however, Young was a middle-aged ex-hippie with a drinking problem.) But whereas Jesse and Luke opted to never solidify the Sammy lineup by drafting in permanent members, Malkmus and Kannberg—after recording *Slanted* as a duo plus Young—added Ibold on bass and Nastanovich on percussion and background vocals. These additional players would form the first incarnation of the group, touring as well as recording 1992's EP *Watery, Domestic*. In 1993, Young was replaced by Steve West, a more reliable (but also less adventurous) drummer who was the same age as the rest of the guys in the band. This is the lineup that would tour and record until breaking up in 1999 (before reforming several times for reunion shows and tours).

Not only had Luke been an early fan of the group—remember how he flipped when he first heard the Drag City version of "Summer Babe" at the Ritz in 1991—but he also met Pavement early in their existence. Pavement spent the autumn of 1992 in Europe and the UK opening for Sonic Youth. Luke was along to keep an eye on a writer who was embedded with Sonic Youth to write a story about them for *Spin*. Luke saw Pavement play about ten shows as part of that tour. He even lobbied them to sign to Geffen. Pavement told him to fuck off but did so politely seeing as how Luke was aligned with Sonic Youth, the headlining band. He didn't take it personally; it was just business. "I think they thought I was just another corporate record company guy," Luke says with a laugh, "which maybe I was."

Jesse had heard Pavement because they were on some of the mixtapes Luke had made him. He liked *Slanted and Enchanted* well enough, but that's about it. He didn't know who was in the band besides Malkmus and Ibold, and he only knew Ibold because he was a bartender at his brother's old restaurant, Great Jones Café.

Because Pavement had been so successful right out of the gate—*Slanted* was heralded as a bona fide classic pretty much as soon as it appeared—Sammy's similarities to the California band were just as quickly viewed as trying to jump

SAMMY

someone else's train. By trying to harness, if not outright hijack, Pavement's shtick, Sammy was seen as attempting to callously catapult themselves to similar success. As convenient or persuasive a theory as that might be, it's not what happened. Sammy sounded like Pavement for the same reasons that Pavement did: both groups recorded quickly and cheaply, leaving their sound raw and ragged. In fact, lots of bands in the early nineties did. As Luke puts it, "Did Pavement make me feel comfortable that you could have a record that sounded like that and still put it out? Yeah, but so did Sebadoh. There were so many records that were sounding like that at the time." Indeed, it had turned into a scene, a sub-branch of indie rock called lo-fi. Adds Jesse, "Had we recorded the first album the way we did *Tales of Great Neck Glory*, in a real studio, [the comparison] probably never would have come up." And in terms of other elements, like the lead electric guitar lines that sometimes meandered over songs, Luke was basically trying to resemble Joey Santiago's playing in the Pixies. That compressed and distorted top line came from songs like "Debaser." "That's what I was copying," Luke says.

Yet another reason Sammy was compared to Pavement had nothing to do with music, but rather was caused by just one word: *babe*. Because Pavement had "Summer Babe," and Sammy later released "Babe Come Down," the mere appearance of the innocuous noun was enough to be mentioned in a review as being supposedly yet another instance of Sammy copying Pavement. Seeing as how everyone from Styx to Bob Dylan to Sonny & Cher has used "babe" in the title of a song, this strikes me as ridiculous (as it should have struck that reviewer). Precedent had even been set in the indie rock scene. On Dinosaur Jr.'s *You're*

Living All Over Me, the track "Kracked" begins "Come on, babe / Come on, set me free." As silly as the situation was, it would have been avoided if Jesse had listened to his brother. After first playing the song for Phil, he suggested Jesse choose a different word. "Which is kind of why I wanted to keep going with it," Jesse admits. "Just to mess with Phil a little bit."

What didn't make sense to Jesse and Luke, in the face of the Pavement comparisons, was how totally different their songs were in approach and subject matter. Whereas Malkmus's lyrics were almost always opaque if not downright abstract or surreal ("Lies and betrayals / Fruit-covered nails"), Jesse's songs were penetrating portraits of losers and lives lived on the margins of society and class. "Sammy was a much more personal band than Pavement," says Jesse. "The lyrics are about real people and characters and stories. Very Long Island, and an analysis of suburbia and going to the city. And Pavement just didn't have any of that." Adds Luke, "Jesse is telling authentic stories as a young, middle-class Jewish person from Long Island. And he's also working in a zone and a terrain that was pioneered by Lou Reed, who grew up fifteen miles from him. It's so deeply authentic to who he is and his life experience, and I don't think anyone can rob him of that or say with prejudice that it's inauthentic. It's his life."

Other musicians and artists were able to spot the more varied connections and inspirations behind Sammy. "I do think the comparisons to Pavement were fair to some degree, but if you really spend time with the songs, you'll find the bands aren't as similar as they might seem at first blush," says Tony Maxwell, the drummer from That Dog who also played and recorded with Sammy. "Jesse's vocals had something in common with Stephen Malkmus to be sure, but I hear more Lou Reed if pressed to make a comparison." Filmmaker Larry Fessenden agrees, adding that what was lost in the Sammy-sounds-like-Pavement kerfuffle was context. "But a bit of history here: Lou Reed was, long before Pavement, doing the sardonic 'talking blues' or whatever his vocal approach was," he says. "I like Pavement and I liked Lou Reed, and with Sammy, it seemed of a tradition: a slight ironic type of singing."

When *Debut Album* came out, Jesse's old college friend Ben Wheelock was subletting Mark Ibold's apartment while Pavement was touring behind *Crooked Rain*. "Pavement was one of my favorite bands at the time, so it didn't feel like an insult to tell Jesse it sounded like them in some ways," says Wheelock. "To me it felt like it shared some of my favorite elements of early Pavement while also containing all of Jesse's and Luke's musical and lyrical idiosyncrasies." Overseas, while the UK music papers certainly made note of it, the comparisons were hardly enough to sink Sammy. "It wasn't Pavement-y enough for them to get slagged off for it," says Billy Reeves, the PR rep for Sammy's label, Fire Records. "It was more New York." For others, it was more about the attitude. "I generally thought Sammy had more interesting songs," says Edward Douglas, the engineer who worked on *Kings of the Inland Empire* and *Tales of Great Neck Glory*. "I think they were having more fun, whereas Pavement always seemed very dour and very laid-back."

For musician Rebecca Odes, things were more complicated. Her band Love Child had played shows with Pavement, and she'd had several amicable encounters over the years with Pavement members Mark Ibold and Bob Nastanovich (one of Love Child's first shows in NYC was with Ibold's previous group, Dustdevils). And then she started dating Jesse. A week after they met, Jesse took her to his brother's office on Tenth Street, sat her down, and played her Sammy's demo tape. "I remember listening on a futon in the dark, thinking, *Oh fuck, I'm in love with a guy whose band sounds like Pavement.* But then the songs were stuck in my head for a week, and I either stopped hearing Pavement in them or I stopped caring." People in the scene, such as Matador's Gerard Cosloy, gave her shit for being in the band, not that she cared. "Artists take things from each other all the time," she says. "I have a lot of resistance to recognizing influence in my own work. This probably both drew me to and was cultivated by this scene that valued originality over audience. Jesse has a very different paradigm going on."

Even though Jesse's and Luke's consciences were clean, the initial—and ongoing—comparisons (especially when phrased as a put-down) rankled the duo. "I was a little surprised how firm that comparison was right off the bat," says Jesse. Luke, who was spending a lot of time with Kurt Cobain during this period, wanted to get his opinion. On his next trip to Seattle, while they sat in Luke's rented Ford Taurus, he played for Cobain a tape of *Debut Album*. "Who knows," recalls Luke, "Kurt was probably being nice, but he said it didn't sound like Pavement to him. He thought it was better than Pavement."

In the end, most music fans, me included, didn't care that Sammy sounded like Pavement. If you liked both bands, those similarities were a good thing. Much like today's algorithms that continuously and automatically pair songs based on a certain harmonic kinship or parallel, our tastes become the stepping stones we use to discover new things.

(*Trouser Press*, after declaring that *Debut Album* sounded like Pavement, added, "That's not really such a bad thing.") Musical inspiration, and the relationships between different groups, forms a gigantic spiderweb that listeners spend their entire lives gleefully crawling around on and exploring. Like New Order? Check out Kraftwerk. Dig Teenage Fanclub? You'll love Big Star. Want something that sounds like Belle and Sebastian? Give Nick Drake a try. To knock one group for sounding like another is churlish, not to mention it misses the point about what music is, why it grows and expands, and how bands are discovered. It should also be noted that Pavement's early work (indeed, that celebrated debut) has long been tagged as being awfully derivative of the British post-punk group the Fall. Examples: "Our Singer" is heavily indebted to "Hip Priest"; "Conduit for Sale!" rips off "New Face in Hell," and "Jackals, False Grails: The Lonesome Era" sounds an awful lot like "The Classical." And Pavement took more than just musical inspiration from the English band. The handwritten words and phrases on the front of *Watery, Domestic* are unmistakably reminiscent of the scribbled language on the sleeve for *Hex Enduction Hour*, the Fall's 1982 LP.

Why is Sammy dismissed and damned for sounding a bit like Pavement when Pavement got off relatively scot-free for their plundering of the Fall? A key difference I think is timing. Most of the material Pavement aped was a decade old by that point, and thus could be seen as "inspiration." Critics out to smear Sammy—and who viewed Pavement both as Sammy's contemporary and peer—saw the sonic similarities as outright theft. As Rebecca Odes puts it, "The past is fair game; influences are everywhere. It's different to be compared to something that's happening now." And even if Sammy's next two releases showed how flawed, tenuous, and just plain wrong the initial accusations were, the slander has managed to stick and linger after all these years.

After meeting on New Year's Eve, Jesse and Rebecca began dating and lived together in an apartment on Avenue A between Twelfth and Thirteenth Streets. With Luke out in Los Angeles, Jesse briefly formed an informal power trio called Metro with Lyle Hysen from Das Damen and Jerry DiRienzo from Cell. He also played bass in Rebecca's solo project, Odes, and he began to meet other New York musicians, such as bass player Michael Galinsky from the group Sleepyhead (Galinsky would later tour with Sammy and Laptop). While all this activity scratched the itch to play music in the wake of Luke's absence, it also made Jesse ask himself questions. *Are Luke and I still a band? Is Sammy something real, or was it just a few days out in Long Island bashing out a handful of tunes?* "It was kind of interesting being apart," says Jesse, before adding, "even though it was annoying."

Out in California, Luke was getting more sophisticated with recording and arranging in his home studio. He even learned to play drums. This meant he could send Jesse musical ideas that were fully fleshed out, leaving Jesse to write lyrics and vocal melodies on top of Luke's increasingly sophisticated musical creations. The fact that *Debut Album* was beginning to get some real attention in both the US and UK told Jesse and Luke that rather than Sammy ending, it was just getting started. Singles were going to need B-sides, so they needed to record more songs. Jesse flew to the West Coast in August to track new material and play a few shows (it would be his first time in Los Angeles). This set the pattern for the next year or so: Jesse would fly out, stay with Luke in Silver Lake, and they'd bash out songs and arrangements in Luke's home studio.

On drums, they drafted in Tony Maxwell from That Dog (the band's name is often stylized as "that dog."). Jesse and Luke had met Tony at Wesleyan when they were freshmen and he was a sophomore. Back then, Tony was playing guitar and singing in a group called Modern Sounds. Stephen Schwartz, who was also in Modern Sounds, would later change his last name to Trask and cocreate with John Cameron Mitchell the musical *Hedwig and the Angry Inch*. Ex–Worrying Thing bassist John Steeb was Mitchell's boyfriend. In 1990, after Tony had moved to drums, he'd occasionally jam with Jesse and Luke. "It was very clear from the get-go that Luke was smart, ambitious, and determined to make things happen for his band," Tony recalls. "He seemed to have an agenda, but at the time I had no idea just how far-reaching it was." Tony found Jesse a bit more accessible socially, and they quickly became friendly. When Tony took a semester off at the beginning of his junior year, Jesse got him a job at Two Boots. Tony would work at the restaurant on and off over the next couple of years. He eventually moved back to Los Angeles, joining That Dog by replacing original drummer Maya Rudolph (yes, *that* Maya Rudolph). That Dog featured Anna Waronker on guitar and vocals alongside sisters Rachel and Petra Haden. Rachel played bass, Petra violin. The Hadens were the daughters of jazz legend Charlie Haden, and Anna's father was former Warner Bros. Records head honcho (and future coworker of Luke's) Lenny Waronker. Tony was a childhood friend, having met Anna's brother, Joey, when he was twelve.

Joey was already a budding drummer (he would later go on to play with Beck, Elliott Smith, R.E.M., and Oasis). Juggling multiple commitments to different bands was not a problem for Maxwell. In addition to drumming for That Dog and Sammy, he was co-leading a group called 9-Iron with Will Baum, who'd been in Love Child. "As far as I was concerned," says Tony of his numerous musical pursuits, "the more bands the merrier."

That Dog was signed to Geffen and their self-titled debut had come out around the same time as Sammy's first album. Once Jesse made it out to Los Angeles, he and Luke rehearsed with Tony, working on new Sammy songs while Tony learned the back catalog. They played a few shows, including a Wednesday night slot at tiki bar Jacks Sugar Shack on Pico Boulevard along with Pony, Lifter, and Crumbox (the nineties were big on one-word band names). When I ask Jesse and Luke who joined them on bass for these gigs, neither can quite recall who it was. All Luke remembers is he had blond hair. This prompts Jesse to add, "Oh, that actor guy!" When I ask Tony the same question, he responds, "I'm embarrassed to say I don't remember who played bass."

The Friday of Jesse's first week in LA, Sammy played a handful of songs live and sat for an interview on the Southern California college radio station KXLU. Tony had a That Dog show that night and was unavailable, so Steve Shelley, who happened to be in town, sat in on drums. Not wanting to further any rumors that Shelley had played on *Debut Album*, Jesse and Luke cryptically referred to him as "Oil City." The trio played seven songs, five from their first LP and two they were set to record the following day. In a brief interview after the performance, when the DJ asks Jesse and Luke, "Are you involved in any side projects?" Jesse's quick answer goes to the heart of the Sammy situation: "*This is the side project.*" Luke further confirms this later in the interview, telling the DJ, "I took the day off to write songs." In terms of future shows, despite speaking about recording a new album the following year, Luke tells the interviewer, "This is it for a while," ominously adding, "[it] could be for forever."

Luke recording bass for Kings of the Inland Empire.
Courtesy of Jesse Hartman.

The next day, Jesse and Luke reunited with Tony at producer Jimmy Boyle's house. Boyle was a New York–born producer who was making a name for himself in Los Angeles working with bands and producers like Red Hot Chili Peppers and Rick Rubin. The year after he worked with Sammy, Boyle won a Grammy for his remixing production on Alanis Morissette's smash hit "You Oughta Know." It was a step up from Michael Corn's basement studio and cassette eight-track, but not by much. Boyle's home setup only offered sixteen tracks and recorded onto one-inch tape rather than the more standard two-inch. Another wrinkle was that, when they got to Boyle's house that Saturday morning, Kill Rock Stars founder Slim Moon was asleep on the couch. The studio also stank of alcohol. Despite these minor setbacks, the session was loose and productive; everyone wore shorts. "I don't think we were so much thinking about it as a freestanding project," says Luke, "we were just like, 'We need more songs to put out more singles for the first album.'" But as the tracks quickly came together, Jesse and Luke began to think of what they were working on as representing something new for the band, something that could stand on its own. The only hiccup was that they didn't like the way Jesse's vocals sounded. But that was okay; Luke knew a guy in New York who could help.

During the early eighties, Edward Douglas had been in a few bands when he lived in Connecticut. He moved to New York in the late eighties to learn about music production and audio engineering. After working at 39th Street Music, he got a job at the newly opened Magic Shop, which had yet to become a renowned Soho recording studio popular with alternative rock bands. He first crossed paths with Luke when Sonic Youth was recording *Dirty* at the Magic Shop. Douglas became friendly with drummer Steve Shelley during those sessions. This led to him working on several releases on Shelley's Smells Like Records, including early albums by Cat Power and Blonde Redhead.

The Sammy tapes were shipped from Los Angeles to New York, even though the Magic Shop was already booked for another session and also didn't have the necessary one-inch sixteen-track tape machine. That wasn't enough to deter Luke. The client was taking off the Labor Day Monday, so Luke secretly rented the necessary machine and had it shipped to the studio. Jesse came in to record vocals and mix the four songs. It was the first time Douglas and Jesse would meet and work together. After Jesse left, Douglas returned all the gear and settings to the way they were before the holiday. However, when the workweek started up again, Douglas's weekend activities were almost discovered. "On Tuesday, the owner of the studio came in and he saw the tape machine that we'd rented, and I was convinced I was busted," says Douglas. "But he didn't ask about it. He assumed it was something for the other session."

With the four songs mixed and ready to go, Jesse and Luke sent them to Steve Shelley. Shelley liked what he heard. More importantly, he felt that the new batch of tunes didn't sound like Pavement. "He was always concerned a little bit about the backlash he got on the first album," says Luke. But this was pointing toward their own sound, a new sound. So rather than relegate the tunes to various B-sides, Shelley offered to put out the material as an EP. It would appear the following year as *Kings of the Inland Empire*.

Jesse was back in Los Angeles that autumn to practice for a short UK tour. This time he didn't come alone. Rebecca Odes made the trip, along with Brendan O'Malley. The two were going to be Sammy's bassist and drummer for the dates. This made sense since they'd formed the rhythm section a few years prior in Love Child, and O'Malley had recently drummed on the Odes track "Meltaway" released that summer as a seven-inch on Merge. And even though Jesse had given Rebecca the impression that Luke could be intense, she was pleased to discover that her boyfriend's musical partner was pretty much the opposite. "I remember being surprised at how much I liked Luke when we met," she says. "His energy and ambition were super fun and infectious."

Jesse outside the Roxy before opening for Teenage Fanclub. Courtesy of Jesse Hartman.

Before the band flew to England, Sammy had a hometown warm-up gig opening for Teenage Fanclub at the Roxy in late November (I was there; both bands were great). As Luke recalls, "That was one of the highlights of the entire experience for me." He'd been an admirer of Teenage Fanclub for years, watching them perform from the side of the stage dozens of times. Now his own band was sharing a bill with them. Not only that, but Geffen's headquarters was just down the street. "There was something insanely fun about walking out of my office and down to the Roxy for sound check. We were two blocks away." It was also a bit nerve-racking. The audience was filled with lots of Geffen staffers there to see Teenage Fanclub, and many of them were unaware of Luke's alter ego as a guitarist in Sammy.

When they all gathered at the airport a few days later to fly to England, Luke had to hop on a quick call for work. He dialed in from a pay phone in the terminal. As the call went long, passengers began to board the plane. Jesse, Rebecca, and Brendan got out their tickets and stood up. The line slowly inched its way forward. Every time it did, Jesse looked around for Luke. He wasn't visible. Jesse, Rebecca, and Brendan boarded the plane and sat down. Passengers ambled down the two rows, finding their seats and stowing luggage. The click of seat belts filled the cabin as flight attendants walked up and down the aisles, handing out blankets and answering questions. Still no Luke. In an era before cell phones and texting, there was no way to know if Luke was sprinting for the gate or still tied up on the phone. All Jesse could do was wait and see if his bandmate materialized. The doors were soon closed, and the plane pulled away from the gate. Luke did not make the flight. Jesse was shocked, but there was nothing he could do. Adding insult to injury, when Luke booked himself on the next flight, he upgraded himself to business class. "A classic Luke/Sammy moment," Jesse says.

Once they all finally reconvened in London (Luke arriving a day late), Sammy was shepherded around town by their Fire Records PR rep, Billy Reeves. As a music-obsessed teenager, the first group Reeves considered his own was Joy Division. Inspired by their drummer, Stephen Morris, Reeves went out and bought a drum kit for forty pounds.

Despite sounding like he was playing margarine tubs, he became adept on the instrument. Years later, when he was in Brighton attending college, he joined the Blow-Up, a gritty band signed to Alan McGee's Creation Records. "That was a real experience in absolute painful failure," Reeves says. He thought he'd joined the glamorous and cool crowd, only to discover a bunch of upper-middle-class kids being supported by their parents. Disillusioned, Reeves returned home. Even though he and his friends were still just in their early twenties, they figured they were too old to get a new group together. By now it was the late eighties, and the Pixies were making a splash in Britain. As Reeves remembers, "Pixies were such a massive influence on the UK indie scene, you can't even fathom it." Inspired by the American group, Reeves and his friends formed Congregation. They sent their demo to BBC DJ Gary Crowley, who played it as part of his show *Demo Clash*. Despite Congregation being, as Reeves admits, "One of about 157,000 groups who were trying to be the Pixies," Fire Records boss Clive Solomon was listening and liked what he heard. Congregation signed with the label, releasing a few singles in 1994 and an album the following year. Within just a few weeks of his band working with Fire, Solomon told Reeves that the guy who'd been handling PR was leaving to work with Garbage. Did Reeves want the job? Even though this meant taking a massive pay cut from his position as a probate genealogist, he took the gig. Reeves would end up working at Fire for three and a half years.

The band would all be sleeping on the floor of Reeves's small flat in Twickenham, about ten miles outside London. A press release Reeves put together to coincide with the trip described Sammy's tunes as "college rock hits to assuage even the most cynical lo-fi veteran." In addition to getting word out about the band, Reeves put together an itinerary for the group that also included tips on getting around the city: *Public transport is good and safe but doesn't run pretty much after 11:30 p.m.* And even though Fire had managed to set up a slate of high-profile gigs and promotional events, including two headlining shows in London, the whole trip was a bit of a budget operation. The band had paid for their own airfare, and Fire was providing only a meager per diem. When I asked Reeves if the label had brought Sammy over to break them in the UK, he just laughed. In an era when even indie groups were spending $100K on videos and getting half-a-million-dollar advances, it would have taken far more than what Fire was shelling out to make that happen.

First on Sammy's itinerary was a Wednesday night show at London's PowerHaus, supported by Melt and fellow Fire band Cottonmouth. Even though everyone in Sammy was catatonic from jet lag, they turned in a strong performance. Reviewing the gig for *Melody Maker*, Dave Jennings called Sammy "a younger, poppier Sonic Youth" and praised their "casual charisma" and "effortless presence." And even though the breakout stars of the year, at least in England, had been Oasis, Jennings asked why anyone would need Oasis when you can have Sammy: "I mean, why put up with a bunch of Mancunian egomaniacs when Sammy do frayed, blurred guitar-pop with so much more intelligence and charm?" (Pavement isn't mentioned at all in the review; other than Sonic Youth, the only artist cited as an influence is Lou Reed.)

On Thursday, Sammy played an in-store at the Rough Trade shop in Covent Garden. Despite being an acoustic set, Billy made sure there was an amp for the bass. Brendan played tambourine.

On Friday, Sammy was slated to play another headlining show, this time at a club in southeast London called the Venue. Instead, they got a call to make a much more high-profile appearance as musical guests on a live TV show called *The Word*, a notorious series that ran from 1990 to 1995 and was especially developed to appeal to the youth of Britain. In Emily Nussbaum's 2024 book *Cue the Sun! The Invention of Reality TV*, she refers to *The Word* as "more debauched than anything on British TV" and "at once innovative and indefensible." In addition to the usual variety program features like celebrity interviews and live band performances, the hour-long show featured a segment called "The Hopefuls," where people would perform outrageous (and usually disgusting or debasing) stunts to get on television (for example, eating a toenail sandwich). Bands got into the act too. When Nirvana appeared on *The Word*, Kurt Cobain announced to viewers that Courtney Love was "the best fuck in the world." Not to be outdone, the following year Donita Sparks from L7 took off her jeans and underwear while performing, resulting in a flash of full-frontal nudity.

That Sammy had a chance to appear on the show was thanks to Beck, whom Sammy was set to open for later in the week in both Manchester and London. Beck, who was having a banner year with the breakout hit "Loser" and his major-label Geffen debut, *Mellow Gold*, had been offered *The Word* but turned it down. A story in the same issue of *Melody Maker* that carried the review of Sammy's show at the PowerHaus outlined the situation. Under the headline "BECK BAILS," the unsigned piece began, "Beck pulled out [of] a scheduled appearance on the opening show in the new series of 'The Word' last Friday (November 25), after the show's producers demanded that his appearance be limited to three minutes in accordance with the rule the show imposes on all musical guests." The BBC also required bands be there all day long, even though they didn't perform until late in the day, and Beck didn't want to have to spend hours and hours waiting to go on.

The night Sammy appeared, additional guests were American talk show host Ricki Lake, British boxer Prince Naseem, John Bobbitt (the guy whose wife cut off his penis), as well as two other musical acts: South African hip-hop band Prophets of Da City and electronic DJ Goldie. There was also a prank segment that feels like an early version of *Punk'd*, in addition to a report on policewomen going undercover as hookers in New Mexico. It was an eclectic mix to say the least. Introduced by host Terry Christian as "the cutest quartet to come out of America since the Monkees," Sammy played a blistering version of "Babe Come Down" to a huge crowd of dancing teenagers, some of whom were wearing fur bikinis. Rebecca Odes rose to the occasion by sporting a hat in the shape of a cat's head. "When I was at art school in Chicago, my roommate Ruth Root and I came up with a project that grafted stuffed animal heads onto formal clothes. I found the cat hat at Patricia Field and bought it as a version of that," she says. "It was the same day I dyed my hair blond for the first time, so the hat became sort of linked to that transition. It felt like the touch of absurdism *The Word* required."

"That was a bananas experience for us," says Luke. "It was a big deal," adds Jesse. "It was four million viewers, and we had never done anything like that. And it's live." It was also the band's eighth or so gig.

On Saturday, the group and Billy Reeves made the five-hour trek north to open for Beck at Manchester University. Sammy couldn't hang out with the headliner since they all needed to be back in London for their Peel session the next day. Legendary DJ John Peel had been asking bands to record four songs for his BBC Radio 1 show going all the way back to 1967. These sessions, which took place at BBC's West London Maida Vale studio, often gave huge boosts to new and even unsigned bands.

Luke at Maida Vale for Sammy's Peel session. Courtesy of Jesse Hartman.

From noon to midnight, Sammy recorded "Babe Come Down"; "Inland Empire," one of the tracks from the summer session at Jimmy Boyle's house in LA; "Slim Style," a new tune that would ultimately appear on their second album; and "Trick Mammoth," a gorgeous slow song that sees Jesse pining for home while Luke goes crazy in the background with his beloved whammy bar. "Trick Mammoth" would appear the following year, in the UK at least, as part of the Fire single for "Majik Man." The band had a blast recording the songs. "We were like, 'This is crazy,'" says Luke. "Our heads were blown."

Spending so much time with the group gave Reeves ample opportunity to get to know Jesse and Luke. More than anything, he couldn't believe that—for young guys supporting their first record—they'd both been in so many bands and had accomplished so much. Reeves was also impressed by how polite the pair were. "They treated everything really professionally," he remembers. And even though Sammy had arrived and were playing as a four-piece, as Reeves explains, "We were pitching them as a duo. Because obviously [Jesse and Luke] were the main guys." This meant that Rebecca and Brendan were often expected to make themselves scarce. "Because I was not supposed to be part of the story," Rebecca recalls, "I was not supposed to be around when the story was being written. I had to leave the room whenever there was media around. I was mostly fine with that." But she sensed that something else also seemed to be part of this strategy; that perhaps adding more people to the group would have upset the somewhat precarious balance that existed between Jesse and Luke. "I also think there was a sense that the dynamic between them needed to be handled carefully, that putting other people in the mix might upset it."

On Monday—their last day in town—Sammy played a lunchtime acoustic radio session before heading to London's Astoria to open for Beck. Seeing as how Beck was on the label that Luke worked for, there were tons of Geffen people backstage. Luke seemed to know them all, and he was totally comfortable and in his element. It was also, thanks to Sammy's recent appearance on *The Word*, a great gig. The crowd sang along and there was a lot of energy for the group in the room. "TV just does that," says Luke. "It creates a weird moment in time. It's like, *Oh, you're a big band because we saw you on TV. So we're going to pay attention.*" Later, at the merch table, there was a line of fans wanting Jesse and Luke to sign shirts. "It was probably my favorite show we ever played," says Luke. Adds Jesse, "It was all much more exciting than being in New York or Los Angeles. It was really fun." Reeves's itinerary instructions to the band for after the show were both paternal and hip: *It would be appreciated that as this is party night that you guys grab the geetars and cop a black cab back to H.Q. for this. All 4 will be able to get in and it'll be about fifteen pounds.*

It had been a great trip. Unfortunately, because Fire hadn't timed the release of the singles, with their debut, "Babe Come Down," having come out months previously, the band couldn't adequately or completely capitalize on their momentum. "Things would have been very different for us potentially in the UK if we had managed to line up 'Babe' with all that promotion," says Luke. Instead, the follow-up, "Hi Fi Killers," did okay, but it didn't make quite the same splash. It wouldn't be the last time Sammy would come tantalizingly close to breaking through.

In 1995, Sammy released *Kings of the Inland Empire* on Smells Like Records in the US and Fire in the UK, an EP made up of the four songs they'd recorded the previous August. The Inland Empire is an area east of LA encompassing the cities of Riverside and San Bernardino. And while it's indeed a huge and sprawling space—home to over four million people spread over 27,000 square miles—calling it an "empire" is a stretch. Ancient Rome was an empire. China's Qing dynasty in the seventeenth century was an empire.

This "Inland Empire" is just one gigantic swath of suburban sprawl hardly different from any of the dozens of others that populate the huge state. That false and almost delusional grandeur was exactly what appealed to Jesse and Luke. It perfectly fit the quartet of songs, some of which were about small-town people imagining bigger lives for themselves, wannabes who were royalty only in their own minds.

This idea bled into the cover art, which was shot by Michael Lavine, a noted photographer who worked with several important bands from the alternative era (Sonic Youth, Nirvana, Smashing Pumpkins). On the front, Jesse and Luke pose as gangsters, sporting brown leather jackets and brandishing pistols (Luke, wearing dark aviator shades, holds his gun in the side-grip fashion made popular by the cop shows and hip-hop videos of the day). And while the title references plastic California, here they're on the mean streets of Manhattan. On the back, the guys—now wearing suits—are all grins and smiles, as if taking a break from the characters they're playing. While the front and back make the duo seem like career criminals in cahoots, in dozens of outtakes, Jesse and Luke point the guns at each other, pistols pushed right up against faces in the style of John Woo's *Hard Boiled*, which had been released just a few years prior.

As playful as the final cover was intended to be, it partially spoke to how the pair felt: embattled, defensive, a little bit pissed off. "We thought we always had a chance to be part of the burgeoning indie rock kind of thing," says Luke, "but we didn't think we'd get the kind of attention we got." Adds Jesse, "It was a really difficult landscape. It was like being in *The Scarlet Letter*. [The indie scene] was really puritanical and quite unpleasant actually at times." What didn't help is that the overall design of the EP was yet another poke in the eye to the scene. Indie bands in the nineties were loath to put themselves on the cover of their records, which was seen as gauche. The vogue was for old Polaroids, handwritten lettering, and D.I.Y. design (something that had indeed shown up on early Sammy releases). They now decided to go against all of that. "I wanted to kind of hark back to the seventies, where it was okay to show your face," says Jesse. They knew that this went against the grain of what was currently popular. As Jesse admits, "That probably just made people hate us more."

The EP kicks off with "Inland Empire." The super-catchy song had been inspired by something that happened to Luke while Jesse was out in LA staying with him in advance of the recording session. Luke had been asked to watch an advance cut of *Pulp Fiction* in the Geffen screening room because Urge Overkill—a group he was working with—had their cover of Neil Diamond's "Girl, You'll Be a Woman Soon" on the soundtrack, and there was some talk at the label about working it as a single. "I didn't know anything about Quentin Tarantino, or the movie," recalls Luke, "and I was super surprised at how good it was." When he got home, Luke told Jesse about the film. They then had the idea to take those hard-boiled *Pulp Fiction*–type characters into the world of Sammy. Jesse, even though he hadn't seen the movie, got the idea immediately. "Inland Empire" was written that night. In the lyrics, the narrator talks about the desire to drive a big car, run red lights, and shoot both a gun and drugs, before admitting that he lives at home with his mom and has never gotten into trouble before. It's all a fantasy, a projection, conformity rather than a life of crime: "I just want to be like you." The track is yet another brilliant character study by Jesse, a sort of mini-film in the guise of a pop song. Luke's Robert Fripp–inspired floating lead guitar line was played with an EBow, a small handheld device powered by a nine-volt battery that uses a pickup and magnet to vibrate strings and create sustain. The following year, R.E.M.'s "E-Bow the Letter" would not only employ a similar sound but name-check the gadget in the title. (And, for the record, Geffen wisely issued "Girl, You'll Be a Woman Soon" as a single; *Pulp Fiction* proved to be a gigantic success, and the song proved to be Urge Overkill's biggest hit.)

Next up is "Majik Man." Luke came up with the chords, and Jesse's lyric is about when he met Rebecca Odes at Two Boots: "You bubbled into my life on a New Year's Eve so nice." During their months living together in the East Village, the area was still a bit rough, with burning garbage cans and an omnipresent ice cream truck that was constantly swarmed by feral kids. "By having such a strong and insanely sweet lyric, it really changed the feel of the song," says Luke. "Jesse was newly in love, and this song captures that energy."

"Teen Tour" is another autobiographical song; it's about the six-week trip Jesse took to Israel when he was in high school. The track, with its rocking instrumental break toward the end, was Steve Shelley's favorite song on the EP. Jesse wrote most of the music, while Luke's lead work consists of him finger-tapping on the Jazzmaster as well as getting more healthy use out of his whammy bar.

Final tune "Cracked Up" was a song that Jesse had worked on in New York with the short-lived group he'd formed called Metro during that weird period after Luke left for LA and Jesse wasn't sure if Sammy was going to continue. When he went out to California in August of 1994, he played it for Luke, and it quickly became a Sammy song. All of Luke's lead guitar work over the top of Jesse's chords was improvised. Also, Jesse and engineer Edward Douglas—after the tapes had been sent to New York—discovered why Luke's guitar sounded so removed and distant: Jimmy Boyle had turned on the wrong mic in the studio, so it was being recorded by an SM57 ten feet away from the amp. Rerecording the vocals at the Magic Shop with Douglas allowed Jesse to push and experiment with falsetto and harmony, paving the way for what Sammy would do on their next album.

Ahead of the EP's release, in January Jesse sent to Fire Records ideas for videos for two of the EP's tracks. In the proposed clip for "Inland Empire," Jesse and Luke would have presented themselves as middle-class schlubs from Great Neck with boring day jobs who trade in their small Honda for huge a Cadillac and swap their nerdy clothes for slick suits and fancy shoes (and a pair of pistols). A stylistic mash-up of movies ranging from recent classics *Reservoir Dogs* and *Drugstore Cowboy* to cinematic staples like *Taxi Driver* and *The Godfather*, the video also would have featured Brendan O'Malley and Rebecca Odes joining Luke and Jesse vamping as a tribute to Factory-era Velvet Underground. The idea for "Majik Man" was much more playful. Jesse, Luke, and Brendan would have played bachelors on *The Dating Game*, the fun but cheesy game show started in the sixties in which a woman chooses from among three potential suitors (none of whom she can see). The bachelorette would have been played by Rebecca, which makes sense seeing as how the song was inspired by her. In the end, and in a twist on the usual format, Rebecca would have chosen all three bachelors. The entire band is then sent on a cruise to the Bahamas, where, thanks to the magic of green screen, all four cavort on the beach. Each video would have been codirected by Jesse and Larry Fessenden, edited by Fessenden, with Rebecca as the set designer. Budgets for each were modest, with "Empire" estimated to cost $5,728 and "Majik" coming in slightly higher (due to the creation of the *Dating Game* set) at $6,604.

While neither clip was ultimately produced, Sammy appeared on TV in late March by playing "Majik Man" live on Jon Stewart's talk show (four years before he became the host of *The Daily Show*). Started as a thirty-minute program on MTV in 1993, when Sammy made their appearance, *The Jon Stewart Show* had expanded to an hour and was in syndication across the country (it went off the air that summer). The lineup was the same as the UK tour from the year before: Odes on bass and Brendan O'Malley on drums. The band had fun taping the performance. It was far less stressful than when they'd appeared on *The Word*, and friends like members of Girls Against Boys and Jesse's brother, Phil, showed up to lend support.

David Daley, reviewing *Kings of the Inland Empire* for *Alternative Press*, cited the usual comparisons to Sonic Youth and the Velvet Underground, as well as Pavement (noting that Sammy might in fact be "a more motivated Pavement," a low bar to leap given how the California band were perceived as *uber* slackers). In the end, however, Daley concludes that Sammy has "the smarts, sense, and taste to filter out the catchiest aspects of their influences."

Less charitably, overseas in *Melody Maker*, writer Everett True—despite recommending *Debut Album* to his readers the year before—didn't so much review the EP as he did slag off the band, calling Sammy a "bunch of corporate cocksucking, pub rock-standard, pseudo-slackers from New York" as well as mocking Luke's "safe job" with Geffen (True seemingly had no qualms about his own "safe job" with *Melody Maker*). Showing that True's petulant outburst didn't accurately reflect the popular opinion, a fan from Lancaster named Catherine who'd been at Sammy's PowerHaus show wrote in with a rebuttal that was printed a few weeks later. After stating that Everett's "excuse for a review appears to have been written by someone who has no journalistic skills whatsoever," Catherine defends the group—and more specifically its singer—from the usual accusations: "They do not rip off Pavement. Jesse Hartman can't help his voice being similar to that of Steve [*sic*] Malkmus and I can hardly see him changing the way he sings to please people like Everett."

Back in the States, after lead track "Inland Empire" started getting spun on college radio, something interesting happened: it also began to get late-night play on KROQ, the influential Los Angeles station that was known as being an alternative rock kingmaker. Once KROQ championed tracks like Beck's "Loser" and Weezer's "Undone (The Sweater Song)," other stations began playing them as well, turning those songs into hits (and giving those artists lasting careers). Luke even heard from a friend of his who was a DJ at KROQ that "Inland Empire" almost got put into full rotation. Once that happens, a major-label deal is all but assured. KROQ had so much power that even *almost* getting put into full rotation could be enough to land a deal. "Whenever you get that close to being added to a major station like that, people take you really seriously," Luke says. "That's like a fucking lottery ticket."

As if on cue, major labels started reaching out. Meetings were set up, and Jesse and Luke had lunches with A&R reps. Almost immediately they ran into a problem. A big one. Luke was director of marketing at Geffen. Why would Warner Bros. or Capitol sign a band that had a member who worked for the competition? Talks went nowhere. They *couldn't* go anywhere, not while Luke worked at Geffen. Luke tried to explore the idea with people at Geffen, but they quickly made it clear they would not be comfortable if he signed with a competitor. He was too visible. His job was too big. In a way, Luke was a victim of his own success. If he'd been some guy in the mail room, it would have been different.

"As you can imagine," admits Jesse, "I was a little frustrated with this situation." Adding to his frustration was the fact that while Luke was pulling down a huge salary, Jesse was still working at Two Boots, dealing with irate customers and staying late into the night along with the dishwashers and busboys. Sure, it was fodder for songs, but was he going to do this forever? "I was on the edge," Jesse says. "I needed to get some money and get out of the restaurant world. And Luke knew that." Jesse tried not to put pressure on his bandmate to make something happen, but he couldn't help it.

Luke, meanwhile, was caught in the middle. He wanted the band to happen as much as Jesse, but he'd seen what had happened to his mom. He remembered what it'd been like to not have money. The two preschools, being ferried back and forth as a kid. The music on that car radio had saved him, and now he had a chance to be one of those bands coming out of the speakers and into someone else's car. Maybe Sammy could even save some young kid's life the way that music had saved Luke's. But at what price? And what if it all didn't work out? Luke hadn't worked hard, and gotten to where he was, only to throw it away.

Jesse and Luke ended up making the only decision they felt they could make: keep things the way they were. Sammy would not sign to a major label. They'd record another album—they'd already been working on songs—and once again they'd send it to Steve Shelley for Smells Like Records.

After working their way up from cassette eight-track to sixteen-track, for their next album Jesse and Luke wanted to make the leap to a professional, twenty-four-track studio. By this time, Luke had spent countless hours in studios with bands. He'd made good use of the time, talking to engineers, learning the gear and what different things did and how they worked. Because of this, he felt confident that he and Jesse could produce the record themselves. Seeing as how Jesse and Edward Douglas had hit it off when they worked together on *Kings of the Inland Empire*, they decided to work with him in the same capacity for what became *Tales of Great Neck Glory*. Jesse had hung out a bit with Douglas socially after working on *Kings*, and Luke joined them when he came to town so they could discuss making the second full-length Sammy album.

When they started making the album, Sammy didn't have a record deal. The contract with Fire in the UK had been for just one album, and the status quo situation with Smells Like was informal; Shelley would listen to the tape, and if he liked it, he'd release it. Without an advance from a label, Jesse and Luke had to pay for the sessions themselves, and to save money, they'd have to record quickly. They scheduled just a week in August to record the whole album, a small amount of time to record an entire LP. Douglas preferred to work quickly, having already recorded and mixed what would become Cat Power's first two albums in just two days. Recording at the Magic Shop wasn't an option this time around since Lou Reed had booked the studio for the entire summer. Instead, Sammy headed up to Big House Recording on Forty-Second Street. Although the live room didn't have quite the same sound as the Magic Shop, they made it work. Jesse was just thrilled to be in a professional setting. Outside of the one day he'd spent redoing his vocals for *Kings of the Inland Empire*, he'd never spent time inside a recording studio.

The sessions were fun but focused. Because they had just a week to get everything on tape, Jesse had each lyric and harmony ready to go, and Luke had all his guitar parts down. Douglas had received demos before getting started, so he was familiar with the material. "It was a pretty laid-back session," Douglas says, "considering we only had five days to record and five days to mix." Even though time was tight, the trio still found room for experimentation, like when Douglas fed Luke's guitar through a Leslie cabinet.

Three different drummers played on the sessions, but they were all people Jesse and Luke had worked with previously. Alexis Fleisig, from Girls Against Boys, guested on three tracks. Brendan O'Malley, who'd been in the most recent touring version of Sammy, appeared on two songs. Michael Corn, Jesse's childhood friend who'd drummed on the first LP, sat in for six tracks. There was always a drum kit miked up and ready to go, and each drummer just came in and did their thing, either recording basic tracks as a power trio or occasionally playing drums to tracks Jesse and Luke had already laid down to a click track. Douglas tried to get full band takes whenever possible, using minimal baffling in the studio to get basic separation between the instruments.

Unless there was a major mistake or flub, most of what was recorded as part of these basic tracks was used as the groundwork for later guitar, piano, and vocal overdubs. At that time, there was no Pro Tools, quantizing, or comping together of tracks.

Paying for the sessions themselves led to some awkward situations, like when Luke had to stop recording a guitar part to talk to the owner of the studio because he was demanding a purchase order for the studio time. Luke explained they couldn't provide a PO; a label wasn't paying for the studio, he was. Then the owner demanded cash. A shouting match ensued. Once that was settled, Luke put back on the headphones and returned to recording his part. He was already feeling a bit frayed since he'd come to New York not just for the Sammy sessions but for Geffen business. With basic tracks done, the trio spent another couple of days mixing the songs at RPM, a studio based out of a huge loft a few blocks from Union Square. In yet another effort to save money, they worked nights.

The album's title, *Tales of Great Neck Glory*, was inspired by the Ed Sanders book *Tales of Beatnik Glory*. Sanders was a colorful figure; a founding member of the anarchist sixties garage band the Fugs, he also edited an arts journal called *Fuck You*. His book *Beatnik Glory* was a multivolume work that chronicled downtown New York City life. Phil Hartman, who had gotten friendly with Sanders, was turning the book into a script when Sammy was recording the album. Jesse knew the book and found a relationship between its stand-alone chapters documenting East Village characters and his own tales of suburban angst. Adapting the title for the Sammy record also made sense because Jesse and Luke were thinking of their new album kind of like a book, with each song as a chapter or story that combined into a cohesive and coherent whole (the sleeve even features a photo of a paperback called *Tales of Great Neck Glory*, and there's an excerpt—written by Phil under the name "Monte Karp"—from the imaginary book in the liner notes). Jesse and Luke saw the title as a further ironic continuation of their EP. Whereas those lovable losers thought themselves to be kings, Jesse was here finding glory in coming of age. As he puts it, "Growing up in the suburbs was like fighting a battle." (The title would later create a headache overseas, seeing as how the average British record buyer had no idea where Great Neck was, nor did they catch the Ed Sanders reference.)

It was a very personal album during a period when, like putting yourself on the cover of the record, that kind of thing was frowned upon. The nineties were an age of intense irony; slacker culture was everywhere you looked. Sammy was not playing in that space. "It made sense to us because we'd grown up with Jonathan Richman and Lou Reed. That was what we wanted to tap into," Jesse says. "The stuff that was going on at the time, the sort of abstract songs about nothing, weren't appealing to me. I wanted to get specific."

When they'd mixed down the tracks and sequenced the record, Jesse and Luke sent a cassette to Steve Shelley. Shelley rejected it, saying it was both "too Bowie" and "too commercial." Jesse and Luke were disheartened to hear this. There was already a bit of tension between the band and the label since Shelley didn't like taking flack over Sammy being compared to Pavement. "He was pretty transparent about that," says Luke. "It was embarrassing for him." And so even though Jesse and Luke were smarting at Shelley's rejection, they also knew that he'd never had any sort of ambition to have a commercial record label (after all, a band on Smells Like was named Fuck), so getting Sammy on the radio was never going to be a priority. And even if a track from *Great Neck Glory* started to take off organically, the same way "Inland Empire" almost got added to KROQ, Smells Like wouldn't have had the infrastructure to capitalize on the momentum.

"I think there was an element of relief," says Luke about Shelley's rejection and the severing of ties with Smells Like. Now they were free to find a home that would push the band and maybe even get them to that next level. Their relief was short-lived, since Jesse and Luke immediately landed back in the limbo they'd found themselves in after *Kings of the Inland Empire* started to generate some heat. Except now there was an added element of catch-22: The majors were wary because Luke worked for the competition, but now Sammy was sitting on an LP that had been deemed too commercial for an indie. Undaunted, Luke dug in and started dubbing copies of the album.

However, before Sammy could sign a deal anywhere, Luke had to let someone at Geffen hear the record. He gave a DAT of the final mix to Roberta Petersen, a legendary A&R rep who had only been with the company for about six months. Petersen got her start in the industry by joining Warner Bros. Records in 1971. By 1977, she was managing the A&R department. Petersen was notable for not only being one of the few females in what was a male-dominated industry but also working in A&R, signing and working with bands. She would later become a vice president, working with alternative acts such as Jane's Addiction and Flaming Lips, as well as groups as diverse as Devo and Dire Straits. (Petersen died in 2019 at the age of seventy-four.)

SAMMY

A day after Luke gave her the DAT, she called Luke to her office and told him she loved the record. Petersen offered an easy solution to Sammy's ongoing conundrum, saying plainly, "Why don't we just put this out?"

The guys were happy, but they also knew it was a double-edged sword. Yes, there'd finally be money, and Geffen was a great label, but it was also going to create issues. Number one was the sheer fact that they were signing to a major. Were they selling their souls? Had they given in to the Man? That being said, if Jesse and Luke were leaving the label owned by Steve Shelley—who was Sonic Youth's drummer—to be on the label that Sonic Youth itself was signed to, how could that brand Sammy as a sellout? "There had been a lot of hand-wringing a couple years earlier amongst indie bands about whether or not to sign to major labels," says That Dog drummer Tony Maxwell. "But by the time Sammy signed to Geffen, the dam had broken and the stigma of 'selling out' had largely dissipated." That might have been one bullet Sammy could dodge, but for Luke optics was always going to be an issue. Was Geffen doing it just to keep an executive happy? "Of course, there were bound to be politics around it," says Dennis Dennehy, the replacement Luke had hired when Alexis Fleisig had stopped temping for the label back in 1992. Dennehy would later be Sammy's publicist at Geffen. "There was no way there couldn't be—both internally and externally. But I don't think there was any thought that we 'had to put it out' because Luke worked at the company." In Jesse's world, working with Geffen was seen as nothing but a win-win. "It seemed to be a confluence of good music, a good look, and amazing industry connections," says Phil Hartman. "They seized the day, as they should've."

Not only did Petersen sign Sammy to the label, but she

didn't ask for any changes to the DAT tape Luke had given her. "Geffen did nothing to change the record," Luke says. What got released is what Jesse and Luke made in a week and which cost $4,000. Ten times that amount was often spent just *mixing* an album. "There's no record in Geffen history that I remember," Luke says, "and I was president of DGC eventually, so I would know, that was made in six days for four grand and that came out on Geffen Records." What made this possible was that Petersen had come from Warner Bros. and the world of Mo Ostin and Lenny Waronker. The culture they'd created was one where artists could be artists and grow at their own speed. The belief was, you sign musicians and performers and let them do their thing. It was as simple as that. Roberta Petersen liked the record, so she put it out.

News of the band's signing to Geffen traveled far and wide, and Jesse was interviewed for a story in his hometown paper, the *Great Neck Record*. Under the headline "Landing a Big Time Record Deal," and accompanying a photo from the *Tales of Great Neck Glory* photo shoot, the article chronicles Jesse's upbringing and includes positive quotes from Hartman about his hometown (he praises its "peaceful, artistic environment"). The piece doesn't mention that Great Neck would be part of Sammy's upcoming LP, or that many of its songs would be a critical look at the community. The town would find out soon enough.

The cover for *Tales of Great Neck Glory* is a perfect mash-up of *Debut Album* and *Kings of the Inland Empire*. The general design of *Debut Album* is reversed: instead of white bars at the top and bottom, on *Great Neck Glory* there are black bars, and the band's name and the name of the LP are once again in red and blue, only reversed from the first album. And whereas the lettering was lowercase for *Debut Album*, on *Great Neck Glory* it's all uppercase. And if the all-caps didn't declare itself enough, the font here is made to look like a neon sign; you can almost hear the sizzle of the gas inside the glass tubes as you stare at it. The photo on the front of *Great Neck Glory* calls back to *Inland Empire*—Jesse and Luke are once again pictured, but this time in close-up. The only clue they're in New York is a yellow cab in the background. Luke here poses in a blazer and skinny tie rather than with shades and a pistol, while Jesse has his arms around a woman's neck in a way that doesn't seem entirely welcome; is he holding her out of love, or is he trying to keep her from running away? The shot is blurry and candid, as if all three have been caught in the act of more than just exiting a taxi. (It should also be noted that Luke sports a near-perfect Brian Jones haircut, while Jesse looks his most Jagger.)

The photo on the back is taken from inside the cab, almost from the driver's point of view. The girl sits between Luke and Jesse. The lighting is harsh. All three have those red dots on their eyes everyone used to have in nighttime photos before those omnipresent digital devices in our pockets learned how to cure that. None of the trio seem happy. Luke looks stunned, the woman's clutching the partition between the front and back seats, and Jesse just looks pissed ("This isn't the way to Florent! You should have taken a right at Gansevoort!"). Are they being taken somewhere against their will? The song titles, in the same all-caps neon font as the front, read like tabloid headlines announcing the latest sordid details of Manhattan debauchery. POSSIBLY

PEKING. CHILLING EXCERPTS. KINGS PT. VS. STEAMBOAT.

Outtake from the Tales of Great Neck Glory *shoot.*
Photo by Marcelo Krasilcic.

That these pictures look so natural and stark, a mix between red-carpet paparazzi and bodega surveillance camera, is a credit to fashion photographer Marcelo Krasilcic, who took the shots. Krasilcic's stated style is to "create photographs that feel like intimate captured moments." He does that perfectly with his work on *Great Neck Glory*. After studying photography at NYU, Krasilcic began showing his work around town: magazines, record labels, galleries. His legwork paid off. Soon he was working with bands such as Everything but the Girl, Soul Coughing, and Edison, as well as seeing his work appear in *Dazed & Confused*, *Interview*, and countless ads. The Sammy pictures were captured during a one-day shoot; they started in the afternoon and finished at night. The indoor shots were taken at the Hotel Carter, a location near Times Square that Krasilcic had suggested. "It was one of the cheapest and most run-down hotels in the area," he recalls. "And they didn't mind photo shoots." Krasilcic used a 35 mm Nikon and Fuji point-and-shoot cameras, and he had help from a crew including stylists, hair, and makeup. Extras were friends of Sammy or the crew. The goal was to make the pictures look like a genuine night on the town.

The overall aesthetic of the sleeve art carried over into the video that was made for the first single, "Neptune Ave." In fact, as Jesse wrote in a treatment for the clip, "The idea behind Sammy's photo shoot was to create a series of Cindy Sherman–esque movie stills for a film that doesn't exist. Now it will!" Jesse directed the video, and it's indeed basically a live-action version of the photo shoot, complete with taxicab, female companions, and hotel backdrop in addition to shots of dancing sailors, a limo driver, room service, chambermaids, and rain-slicked Manhattan streets. Luke also plays three-card monte with a couple of girls, and Jesse writes on a typewriter. There's a great scene early on of Luke in the back of the cab, and in the breath-fog of the taxi's window you can see he's scrawled DGC—the name of their record company, and his employer—on the glass. Brendan O'Malley plays drums for a sequence where Sammy performs in the hotel's lobby, but no one's on bass.

The finished film is faithful to Jesse's treatment, with a few exceptions. The plan was to have subtitles appear in English and French at various points "to decipher wacky bits of dialogue (not the song lyrics) throughout." Plus, in the original ending, the frame was going to freeze as the words TO BE CONTINUED appeared on-screen (in order to, according to the treatment, "[add] a dose of suspense for the next video").

The video was shot at an old, dilapidated hotel in New

York called the Roosevelt. Sammy had the run of the place because it was being renovated. This lent the shoot a surreal air. "It was like *The Shining*," says Jesse. "It was completely empty." The video was produced by some college friends who had a production company named Other Pictures, and the cinematographer was Michael Spiller. Jesse had worked with Spiller on that Helmet video all those years before. Spiller had since gone on to shoot videos for Smashing Pumpkins and Sonic Youth, as well as being Hal Hartley's cinematographer. Some of the people in the video were also in the photo shoot. "It was a big filmmaking day for me," Jesse says. He'd never directed anything on that kind of scale before. There was a decent budget, and adding to the overall stress, Geffen people were on hand to make sure everything went smooth.

At the end of the daylong shoot, everyone went for a steak dinner at the Old Homestead restaurant on Ninth Avenue, an outing which got noticed by the *New York Post*. Apparently, the eatery was also a favorite of Axl Rose, who was infamous for dropping wads of cash while dining with an entourage. Jesse and Luke, not so much. In a short piece in Neal Travis's column headlined "Great Guns for Sammy," Travis scoffed, "Where Guns 'N Roses used to drop $15,000 or so at post-concert parties, the tab for Sammy was a paltry $600." Despite the ribbing, it was all a far cry from Larry Fessenden's no-budget clip for "Everglade" shot just two years before.

Looking back, Jesse and Luke acknowledge that the splashy video with lots of extras was yet another thing that rubbed people the wrong way. A day after the video first aired on MTV (which it did quite a few times, appearing on the station's popular alternative music show *120 Minutes*), Jesse was back at work at Two Boots. (Sure, he was a musician signed to a major label, but the cash had yet to arrive.) A grumpy regular came into the pizza place and told Jesse he'd seen the video the night before, quickly adding that it had made him want to vomit. "The last thing this guy wanted to see was me prancing around with a bunch of models in my underwear looking like a rock star," says Jesse. "That gave me an indication that we had already pissed off some people."

It was just one more thing that fed the perception that Sammy was nothing more than well-connected rich kids just having a laugh. And while surface aspects of that accusation rang somewhat true (Great Neck, Wesleyan, high-powered job in the record business, restauranter brother with famous friends), the facts on the ground didn't bear that out. "We made the record for Smells Like Records, which was a very small indie," says Luke. "It's not Merge, it's not Touch and Go, it's not Matador. This is an indie with no employees. It's just Steve running it in Hoboken when he's home from tours." When Shelley rejected the album, Jesse and Luke turned to Geffen because there was no other choice; it was necessity, not nepotism. Still, the overall impression of privilege proved hard to shake. "I remember when a Sammy poster went up in Tower Records," Jesse says. "Someone scribbled on Luke's face, 'Nice work if you can get it.'"

Great Neck Glory is a more accomplished and mature record than *Debut Album*. The LP's eleven songs are simultaneously cinematic and literate, coming across—if not quite a concept album—as a cohesive work not unlike the paperback book also named *Tales of Great Neck Glory* seen in both the liner notes and the video. What grounds and unites the various tracks is how they're all rooted in places and people. In addition to name-checking five New York–area locations or towns (Oyster Bay, Neptune Avenue, Hackensack, Kings Point, the East River, Strathmore), there are seven named characters across the LP: Cathy, Charley, David, Debbie, Elizabeth, Marty, and Scott. Jesse's hero Lou Reed did the same thing, whether that meant naming records after places local and international (*Berlin, Coney Island Baby, New York*), or peopling his tunes with invented personalities who became the protagonists of his sordid tales (Lisa, Stephanie, Jack, Jane, and so on). But unlike Reed, who hated Freeport, the Long Island suburb he came from, Jesse—even in his mid-twenties—was looking fondly if not with some apprehension at Great Neck. "There was always a kind of embarrassment about being from Great Neck because it was known to be kind of wealthy and Jewish and gaudy and shallow and silly, and so you were always hiding it," he says. "You weren't proud to be from Great Neck." His parents, however, were indeed proud. If you managed to move to Great Neck, you'd made it. American Dream achieved. Jesse could only look at it all, bemused and ever-so-slightly ashamed. "You grow up being a little embarrassed by the place you came from." He worked out his feelings in songs, embracing and confronting all the contradictions. For Luke, who hailed from Waspy Rochester, he grew to have an appreciation for Great Neck, and he understood Jesse's take on the place. More importantly, he recognized that Jesse's experience was worth writing about.

Sonically speaking, the album travels over a large range of styles and moods—from rockers to ballads and catchy singles with memorable choruses to piano-driven mood pieces. The stylistic range of the LP is even more impressive since the guys made it over such a short period of time and with limited resources. Sure, Luke had an extensive guitar collection and a lot of gear in his home studio back in California, but all he had with him in New York was his Jazzmaster, which he'd brought on the plane, and a box of pedals he'd shipped from LA (courtesy of the Geffen FedEx account). All the bass on the album was played on a borrowed Fender Precision played through an Ampeg B-15, and most of Luke's guitars went through a Vox AC30.

The album kicks off with "Possibly Peking," a sort of spiritual sequel to the previous year's "Inland Empire." Luke once again uses an EBow, and the groove shows how tight Jesse and Luke had become as a performing unit. "I think the bass and rhythm guitars really sound like one sonic entity," says Luke. The song also shows how Jesse's and Luke's varied influences combined to make a sound that was their own. Jesse was channeling "Strange" by Wire, whereas Luke had in mind "In Like Flynn" by Girls Against Boys (which was a good thing, considering GVSB's Alexis Fleisig plays on the track). Lyrically, the song's about someone named Charley who's lost literally and physically. A petty criminal on the run, he might be in Alaska, Marrakech, or Peking. And yet as dangerous as Charley's flight from justice and his own demons may be, just like the mama's boy in "Inland Empire," Jesse's narrator longs to be part of that world, wondering, "You think they'd let us tag along?" Charles Bukowksi famously wrote, "Some people never go crazy. What truly horrible lives they must lead." This song speaks to the same desire to go wild, only Jesse's characters, locked in the straitjacket of their middle-class upbringings, can only fantasize about a life of crime: "The possibilities we dreamed made our night so much more interesting." Sometimes just dreaming about going crazy is enough. Grammy-winner Tom Lord-Alge, who's worked with groups such as Weezer, Taking Back Sunday, and the Rolling Stones, did a remix of "Possibly Peking," slated to be the LP's third single, but it was never issued (nor can Jesse or Luke today find a copy of it).

"Encyclopedi-ite," the story of Jesse's brother's influence on his life, and the somewhat limiting effect it might have had on his emotional growth, is next on the album. As Luke puts it, "This is the song where Jesse finally confronts his brother and the unique relationship with his cultural Sherpa." Being shown the path is great, but sometimes you want to have the adventure for yourself, even if that means taking wrong turns. Production-wise, the track is light-years beyond what Sammy was doing just two years before in Michael Corn's basement. This was mostly thanks to Luke and what he'd learned from being in the studio with groups or close listening to recent records. Here, an acoustic guitar part acts almost as percussion throughout the song, a technique Luke admired on *Siamese Dream*. "Jesse will hate that as he was much more interested in David Bowie at this point and didn't even really listen to contemporary records. I was the opposite," Luke says. "I was obsessed with what people were doing in the studio." He was also willing to learn from the masters. Luke's lead guitar line was meant to sound like the melody from "Here Comes the Sun."

While Sammy was on a West Coast tour supporting *Great Neck Glory*, they shot home footage for a video that Jesse only got around to piecing together thirty years later. In between Jesse lip-syncing the lyrics while standing on Los Angeles's Sunset Boulevard, the clip shows the usual slices of tour life: doing laundry, logging miles in a van, playing shows, dealing with fans, recording interviews. But Jesse's contemporary editing of these lost scenes points to an added influence beyond just Phil: Luke. In the video, when Jesse sings, "I absorbed like a sponge everything that you'd done," we see Luke in his office at Geffen, pacing and working the phones. Sure, Phil showed Jesse the requisite records and bands to be into, but he could never be the peer and partner-in-crime that Luke later became. The next line in the song is "I followed your lead; I never once disagreed." Sammy was a band that was remarkably light on drama and intrapersonal conflicts. Maybe this speaks to the short duration it existed for, combined with the fact that Jesse and Luke had a foundation of being friends for almost ten years before they had to spend all that time together in the van. For whatever reason, the pair got along. "Luke and Jesse always seemed like great foils for each other, both musically and personally," says Tony Maxwell. "Amazingly, I never recall there being much tension between them."

Like "Rudy" from *Debut Album*, third track "Slim Style" is an homage to a colorful character Jesse met at Two Boots. Joseph "Count Slima" Williams is a legendary East Village fixture, a prolific poet and pool player who can often be found at a bar called Sophie's. Born in Queens in 1949, he started working at Two Boots when it first opened in 1987. He worked there for decades, only leaving when it transitioned from being a restaurant with a bar to more of a takeout by-the-slice pizza place. He still lives in the neighborhood, and Two Boots has since honored him by naming a slice after him (bacon, meatballs, and ham on a Sicilian crust). "I spent a lot of time with him at the restaurant," says Jesse. Sometimes they'd even go out after work, Slima taking him to social clubs and after-hours joints

Jesse didn't know existed. Slima was also part of the *Great Neck Glory* photo shoot; you can see him in the liner notes wearing a cape (a bit of sartorial flair Jesse mentions in the song: "She loved that cape you wear"). References in the lyrics to "passing through walls" refer to Slima's stated belief that he's from another planet, although Jesse was never sure how seriously to take those claims (meaning, whether Slima believed it; Jesse himself was pretty sure Slima *wasn't* from another planet). Some of that behavior may have been caused by a brain tumor that went undiagnosed for years. Jesse wrote the lyrics to "Slim Style" in one day back in Los Angeles, in November of 1994, when Sammy was preparing to fly to London. They played it during the trip, working out the arrangement and recording it as part of their Peel session. They performed it for an audience a few days later when they opened for Beck. As much as they love what's on *Great Neck Glory*, according to Luke, "We never quite got back to the innocence of the Peel version." The chorus guitar line is another example of Luke repeating a melodic phrase over and over as the chords change below. "That trick still kills me to this day," he says.

If "Slim Style" could be considered Sammy's most beautiful song (which I find it to be), a case could be made to categorize "Neptune Ave. (Ortho Hi Rise)" as their most gloriously catchy. Described by Jesse as "an ode to the hard-boiled character I wish I'd been or could be, but don't really have the balls to be," the track was never issued physically as a single in the US, but Fire Records issued it in the UK. Neptune Avenue, located in the Brooklyn neighborhood of Coney Island, is a long street that runs parallel to the beach. The song was originally named just "Ortho Hi Rise," a classically opaque Luke creation (it came from a sign that read ORTHO on a high-rise building he would drive by on Beverly Boulevard on his way to the Geffen offices). The band rechristened the tune "Neptune Ave." when they figured it'd be a single (relegating "Ortho Hi Rise" to parentheses).

In the song, the narrator longs to give life to an imaginary friend, a "hard-boiled" type who has all the nerve and street smarts that they themselves lack. And whereas the protagonist of "Shoot It Around!" boasts to his companion how he's going to "Show you my town," here the wish is reversed: "I wish you could . . . show me the town." The narrator also wants their fantasy companion to be real so he can subject them to a relentless interrogation, asking about all the things that have happened to them, including the most important question of all: "How'd your life ever take such a slide?" Sure, walking on the wild side *looks* fun, but there's a price to pay. The music was a combination of parts written by Jesse and Luke. "Maybe our style was we each were writing choruses," says Luke, "and then we'd put them together and call mine a verse." The song's Peter Hook bass line was inspired by Luke's love of Rochester group Absolute Grey, which is where he first heard the technique of playing high notes rather than low notes on the instrument to cut through the sound (R.E.M.'s Mike Mills did the same thing, as did Lou Barlow in Dinosaur Jr., only Barlow did it LOUDER). It wasn't until years later Luke realized that Absolute Grey had taken the idea from Joy Division. The EBow makes another prominent appearance (Luke admitting, "Yes, I do love 'Heroes' by David Bowie. Am I not human?!"). This is the first song where Michael Corn, Jesse's old friend from Great Neck—and former middle and high school bandmate—makes an appearance (he drums on more than half the LP). His playing throughout *Great Neck Glory* is stellar, and Edward Douglas does an amazing job here and elsewhere recording the drums. Not only is this perhaps the poppiest song the band ever wrote, but it perfectly encapsulates everything Jesse and Luke were trying to do with the project. As Luke puts it, "This song sounds like Sammy to me."

For "Buckle-Up Sunshine," Luke wrote most of the music ("You can hear in the intro we were thinking about the Cars"). The lyrics tell the true story of a fourth-grade friend of Jesse's who disappeared suddenly. "His dad was in trouble with the law," he remembers, "and they ran off to Florida in the middle of the night." The Great Neck dream had come to an end: The colonial home was duly sold, along with all its furniture. Jesse was never able to track the friend down to see what had happened. In the song, the narrator fears that the same thing might happen to him, either as a kid who has to move or an adult who breaks the law ("I was afraid of a conspiracy / Afraid of what I would turn out to be"). British neo-mod group Friends of the Bride (which counts former Fire Records PR rep Billy Reeves as a member) sort of covered the song as a seven-inch in 2007. They rewrote the lyrics to be a tale of a massive house party but kept some of the choruses and the general tune (physical versions are hard to come by, but the band made a video that you can find on YouTube).

Not only is next track "Blue Oyster Bay" another true tale from Jesse's life spent in and around Great Neck, but the way the narrative unspools makes it feel as much like a short story as a song. It's about a night out during his college years when Jesse borrowed the family car and drove to Oyster Bay, a town about twenty miles from Great

SAMMY

Neck, to see a cover band Michael Corn was playing in (the reference in the second line to the group's repertoire of "fusion and funk" points out how different Corn's tastes were to Jesse's or Luke's; Corn preferred Weather Report to the Velvet Underground). "I drank too much and got kicked out of the bar," recalls Jesse. There's a great touch in the liner notes where, after the printed line "Yeah, Debbie called your mother a bitch," in parentheses, it says, "No she didn't!" as if a kind of aside. The sound at the beginning of the track is the metronome that Jesse and Luke played to since Corn wasn't on hand to provide drums when they laid down the basic tracks. "I remember being in the studio when Jawbreaker made *Dear You* for Geffen," says Luke, "and they had done that, so it seemed like a good idea." This is also the first of two songs from the album Corn would play on that were inspired by him. And since this was recorded late in the sessions (which is to say, toward the end of the week), the guys were running out of time, so there are fewer harmonies, and the track boasts a slightly sparser production than elsewhere. The title is, of course, a pun on the name of the Long Island band Blue Öyster Cult, who were big in the seventies (if that seems like an uncool reference, keep in mind that Patti Smith dated Allen Lanier from the band, and R.E.M.'s Michael Stipe was such a fan as a teenager he used to wear a Blue Öyster Cult medallion).

Listed as "Chilling Excerpts" on the back of the album, the liner notes show the full title of the next track to be "Chilling Excerpts Bare the Soul of a Monster." As Jesse says, "That sounds like a Luke title, or a direct quote from a headline in the *New York Post*." The song, which is reminiscent of Lou Reed's "Billy" from *Sally Can't Dance*, looks at how two childhood friends have diverged, taking different paths in life. Here, while the narrator left town to go to college, his friend David "chose to stay at home." The song is inspired by Corn, who remained in Great Neck after high school. There are additional biographical aspects; the line "He's afraid there aren't enough doctors" is a reference to Corn's mom, who was a hypochondriac. While Jesse's heart was in the right place when he penned the lyrics—he meant it as a love letter of sorts to the resolve of an old friend—that's not the way it was received. "I don't know what part of a monster I ever was to him," Corn says. When he went to the studio to play on the track, Edward Douglas divulged that Jesse had told him to mute the lyrics so Corn wouldn't know the song was about him. Corn just shrugged and replied, "I already know, let's go, let's play. Whatever." Despite the misunderstanding, Corn's involvement in those first couple of bands saved Jesse. "I was kind of a jock and a budding popular guy in fifth and sixth grades," he says, "and then I veered off of that to these quirkier characters and became an artsy music guy."

Clocking in at a mere 2:32, "Red Lights Flashing" is the shortest song on the album. Whereas earlier track "Majik Man" had chronicled the beginning of Jesse's relationship with Rebecca Odes, here he's documenting its end. Scenes of domesticity (cooking artichokes, cleaning the apartment, toasting with cocktails) are juxtaposed with him leaving ("I grab my coat and head for the door"). He also came up with the music. "Jesse wrote all of this song, including all the guitar parts—I may not have even played anything on it but bass," says Luke. As the song sputters to a climax after two minutes, there's a tape splice and it kicks back in for another couple of frenetic bars, Jesse wailing away on piano in addition to the distorted guitars and vocals.

"Anything" is a song about adolescent love, as well as the need to escape. After the teenage narrator proclaims he's willing to debase himself with a variety of suburban chores (washing windows, waxing cars) just to get close to the object of his affection, he then wails, "I am so bored of this summer." Sure, he's in love, but it's also hot out and there's nothing good on TV. You get the sense that the declaration "I would do anything for you" is only applicable until September comes and he goes away to college. For all Jesse's similarities to Lou Reed as a singer-songwriter, this is where he most *sounds* like the Velvet Underground front man, channeling the vibe of laid-back tracks like "I Love You." It's also one of the very few Sammy songs where piano is the main instrument.

The record begins to head into the final stretch with the high-energy track "Horse or Ballet?" When I ask Jesse point-blank what the lyrics mean (Separate the sheep from the goats? Apricot jelly? Electric shock? What the fuck?!), he plainly answers, "I don't know." He thinks some of it might have come from a book of expressions he had. He would use the book to give him prompts and ideas when writing. Luke encouraged this, pushing his bandmate toward nonlinear songwriting and surreal tales, even if it didn't come naturally to Jesse. "I'm not inclined to write this way," he says. Luke's solo was inspired by Tom Verlaine's on "Marquee Moon." There's also a lot of wah-wah pedal and Luke's liberal use of the whammy bar on his Jazzmaster. What does it all add up to? Is it too much? Horse or ballet? You decide.

That the final track on *Tales of Great Neck Glory* is "Kings Point vs. Steamboat" makes perfect thematic sense since it's the one that most speaks to the town where Jesse grew up, not to mention it reinforces the album's themes of class and status. Kings Point is the wealthy area at the tip of Great Neck. Steamboat is like the wrong side of the tracks, the more down-and-out area. Strathmore, where Jesse grew up, was kind of in between (before the song starts, as Luke counts in the tune, you can hear him refer to it as "Kings Point versus Strathmore"). Living amid these extremes gave Jesse a unique vantage point of what was happening all around him. "My town was a hard place to grow up in if you weren't at the top of the chain." In the song, the narrator—someone from Kings Point—is consoling a kid from Steamboat. This sounds nice, until you realize it's being done from a position of patronizing privilege (the narrator assuring his affluent friends that, sure, the interloper might be a hick, "but that's part of [his] charm"). This makes the kid angry, and he begins to shout and lose control. Of course, behavior like that gives the wealthy inhabitants of Kings Point the vapors. The police are called, and the noisy hooligan is given a stiff fine for offending the delicate locals. Late in the song, when the narrator asks, "What happened to that kid next door?" it's a call back to "Buckle-Up Sunshine" and "Possibly Peking," with their tales of townspeople disappearing from Great Neck one step ahead of the law. There's a bit of self-awareness and ownership, the narrator conceding that he and his rich cohorts were "oh so mean" to the poor kid. In the end, the outcast who had been persecuted in Great Neck goes on to be a merchant marine, where he then dishes out punishment to the unfortunate souls who serve under him. The cycle of abuse, which began in Great Neck, continues. "There's a sadness to some of this stuff," says Jesse. Thinking about how lyrics and ideas like this might have fit into the indie rock of 1996, he continues, "I've never really analyzed the lyrics of other bands of this era. I don't know what they were writing about, but I don't think it was something like this." Production-wise, the drums on the song once again sound amazing. "Corn played drums, and you can really hear how good he was," says Luke. "There's a lot of drum fills, and you hear how comfortable he was in Sammyland." The instruments are hard-panned, with Luke's bass on the left and Jesse's rhythm guitar on the right (in addition to a sonar-esque high piano note that ping-pongs back and forth between both channels). Jesse's vocal is doubled, and Luke provides some effective falsetto background vocals in the second verse. As the song ends, Jesse croons over and over, "Let's make our getaway." Very fitting for the last words on what would be the band's final album.

Reviews for *Tales of Great Neck Glory* were even stronger than for *Debut Album*. Sure, there were the inevitable—and snarky—Pavement mentions, but more often than not Sammy was compared to the Velvet Underground rather than to the California slackers. In addition, Jesse was increasingly being singled out for the wit and depth of his lyrics. "He makes the small-town dramas come alive without patronizing the participants," wrote Dave Jennings in *Melody Maker*. Continuing the theme, *CMJ* praised Jesse's words as "clever and cryptic" and stated that "the band cranks out super-catchy tunes that will make your lo-fi hum contentedly." The *NME* called *Tales* a "languid, crafty gem," awarding it a seven out of ten, while *Puncture* said that Sammy "pen terrific tunes while exuding a boatload of personality." Legendary critic Robert Christgau gave the LP an A- in *The Village Voice* and called Jesse and Luke "alt-rock everyboys," praising the band for being "about hedonism not idealism, choice not necessity."

Raves aside, Sammy's second album entered a very different world and atmosphere from its first. Now that the band was on Geffen, they were no longer slugging it out in the low-stakes world of indie rock and competing with groups on Teen-Beat, Shrimper, or K Records. Sammy was in the big leagues. Other bands, and some people in the industry, took this as Jesse and Luke punching above their weight. "If we had been fortunate enough to stay on Smells Like Records, it probably could have continued that momentum of people actually championing us," says Luke. "But once we got on Geffen, we were basically getting in their ring. And then it was like, 'No, wait a minute, you guys are junior varsity. We love you, you're funny junior varsity players, but you're not varsity. So now you're going to get into *our* arena and *our* playing field and try and fuck with us? You guys are over.' It was very competitive."

Things had also changed in the world of alternative rock since the early nineties. The Nirvana gold rush had been over for years, and it was getting harder for just any downtown NYC band to get a major-label deal. What was selling in 1996 was large-scale ROCK: Rage Against the Machine, Pearl Jam, Soundgarden, Bush. With groups like this topping the charts, it was difficult for a band like Sammy who loved Television and the Velvet Underground to gain much traction. Luke's association with Geffen—which you might think would have been an asset—continued to work against him. "All the press people knew Luke and knew him as a publicist at a major label," says Dennis Dennehy, who worked with Luke at Geffen. "And even though he worked indie-leaning records, he still worked at a major label."

Another timing aspect that didn't help Sammy was that

SAMMY

Geffen, despite its success with Nirvana and others, had struggled with a few alternative acts in the mid-nineties. The label had spent a lot of effort to build an audience for Urge Overkill's 1993 major-label debut *Saturation*. Despite being a solid album, *Saturation* failed to connect in any real way, and the band's 1995 follow-up *Exit the Dragon* fared even worse. Weezer had managed to break through in 1994, but that had hardly been an immediate success. And even though the group's sophomore LP, *Pinkerton*, is today seen as a classic, it flopped when it was first released, savaged by critics and not selling anywhere near the band's debut.

Sammy was hardly the only Geffen group struggling to break through. That Dog, with Tony Maxwell on drums, who had played on *Kings of the Inland Empire*, was also having a hard time. The group was hoping to gain a wider audience with the release of their third album, *Retreat from the Sun*, an LP that Luke had been involved with from start to finish. Even though they were dealing with some internal tension among its members, the band was prepared to tour and promote the record. "Unfortunately, our efforts coincided with the changes going on at Geffen," says Maxwell. In 1995, there'd been a huge shift among Geffen's senior leadership, leading to a mass exodus that would later include David Geffen himself. Gary Gersh, who'd signed Nirvana, left for Capitol. Tom Zutaut, who'd signed Guns N' Roses, left to start his own label. Luke had been feeling the rumblings of the corporate shake-up even as he and Jesse were recording *Great Neck Glory*. "After an initial burst of support," says Maxwell, "we suddenly felt the rug pulled out from under us." They were called into the office of label president Eddie Rosenblatt. Rosenblatt explained that Geffen only had resources to continue promoting That

Dog or labelmates Veruca Salt. And they were going with Veruca Salt. "That was pretty much the final nail in the That Dog coffin right there." Bands were seeing how the kind of success that Weezer and Beck had achieved was rare. Not everyone was going to have a career or hits. "I think there was an inevitable letdown for a lot of us alternative or indie artists who got signed to major labels during that era," says Maxwell, "fueled by the false expectation that we could have lasting success."

Another thing that struck these bands was just how fast things come could crashing down. When Dennis Dennehy started at Geffen, Bryn Bridenthal—the woman who had hired Luke right out of college—told him, "We're very good at burying our dead quickly." If a record wasn't connecting immediately, getting the right kind of feedback in terms of radio, sales, and MTV airplay, that was pretty much it. Game over. Given Luke's involvement in the industry, he was smart enough to know what was happening. Every day he was in marketing meetings where they looked at sales figures. He met with programmers, MTV executives. He knew how to look at the data, and he knew how the label thought about bands. And even though he could tell that the numbers weren't looking good for *Great Neck Glory*, it was out, and they had to promote it. Sammy went on tour.

Rounding out the lineup was Sleepyhead's Michael Galinksy on bass and Michael Corn on drums. Despite having been part of the earliest incarnation of Sammy, Corn had never toured with the band. He was sure this was partly due to his appearance. "I kind of looked like Kenny G," Corn says, referring to a period when he was growing out his dark, curly hair. "Not by my intention, I just did." Jesse did not want Kenny G to be Sammy's drummer. Corn remembers Jesse telling him, "If you agree to get your hair cut, you're coming on this tour with me." Corn cut his hair. But the rock-and-roll makeover didn't stop there. "Jesse also took me shopping for stage-worthy clothes at a vintage place in Brooklyn," Corn says, "which I actually rather enjoyed."

Michael Corn on the Tales of Great Neck Glory *tour.*
Courtesy of Jesse Hartman.

Most of the shows were on the West Coast (including eight in California), with just a handful back East. Sammy was playing small venues, bars and clubs that held an average of three hundred people. And even though Sammy had a big van, they didn't have roadies, so the musicians had to load their own gear in and out whenever they played. At Anaheim venue Linda's Doll Hut, a tiny spot that held just 120 people, the bar was open all day and the band had to load in their gear while patrons sipped their drinks. They also didn't stay at fancy hotels. Along the way, Luke had booked as many promotional opportunities as possible: in-stores, radio interviews, press, anything that would help get the word out (glimpses of this can be seen in the "Encyclopedi-ite" video). A highlight of the first leg of the tour was when they were part of Live 105's BFD festival in June. Held at Northern California's Shoreline Amphitheatre, Sammy played alongside Garbage, No Doubt, Lush, Afghan Whigs, and a dozen other high-profile bands. "During that show at BFD, I did this one random little drum fill, and it came off really nicely," remembers Corn. "In the middle of singing Jesse looked back at me and was like, *That was awesome.*" The West Coast shows were all well attended and spirits were high, even if everyone was working hard; they also didn't have a tour manager, which meant Luke had to be behind the wheel for an all-night drive from San Francisco back to LA after a show at Bottom of the Hill.

After a short break, they gathered for a brief run of East Coast dates: New York, Providence, Cambridge. By now, it was slowly sinking in that *Great Neck Glory* was not doing well. Other than a sold-out show in Manhattan at Brownies, playing to a hometown crowd made up of friends, most of the last run of gigs was depressing. The worst was a show at Club Babyhead in Rhode Island. In a room that held 525 people, only forty-five were in attendance. Jesse and Luke couldn't help but wonder, *Is this what the future holds? Playing to a few dozen people and pulling all-nighters driving the van?*

For Luke, who knew the business side of things, the writing was on the wall. "There was no question in my mind at that point that we were going to get dropped." He saw the airplay. He'd talked to the salespeople. They were all his peers. And the verdict? "Our record at Geffen was DOA within a month and a half of it coming out," Luke says. "And I knew that you can't resuscitate a record like that. You just can't. It doesn't happen." Even though there'd been plans to tour Japan and Europe over the summer, the dates were canceled.

Another factor that doomed the band is that, shortly after *Great Neck Glory* came out, Luke left Geffen for DreamWorks, the new boutique company that was being started by industry heavyweights Steven Spielberg, Jeffrey Katzenberg, and David Geffen. Luke had been wanting to make the move to A&R from PR and marketing for a while, and he felt the best way to do that was by following David Geffen to his new company. More importantly, Geffen had asked him to go.

"To make that jump was a big commitment for me," says Luke, "and it wasn't one I was going to do where it looked like I also had a side hustle." David Geffen had even pulled Luke aside and, referring to his involvement in Sammy, asked him, "What in the fuck are you doing?" This took place during a meeting with just Luke and Geffen at Steven Spielberg's Amblin offices, a bungalow decked out in Southwestern decor on the Universal lot. In its early days, the three DreamWorks founders worked out of these offices. Luke was taken aback, and for good reason. In Nicole LaPorte's 2010 history of DreamWorks, *The Men Who Would Be King*, she writes about Geffen's reputation around town: "Scary David, Mad David, and, most of all, Vengeful David stories are plentiful in Hollywood. Those who know Geffen personally do not bother to deny his ability to frighten." Geffen's point, no matter how it may have been delivered, was nonetheless positive; what he was saying was that Luke needed to focus. "You can be good at one thing," Geffen added, "but you can't be good at three. And you're lucky if you can be great at one thing." His point was crystal clear: Quit playing rock star and focus on your day job. Even though Luke was shaken, he also knew this meant he had Geffen's endorsement. "You have a lot of promise," Geffen had told him. "I'm going to back you. You're going to be on Team David Geffen."

When Luke told Jesse he was leaving Geffen, he also plainly stated that the label wasn't going to keep the band if he jumped ship to another company. "We knew that signing to Geffen could have its ups and downs," says Jesse. "So it wasn't shocking to me when Luke decided to leave." Jesse didn't feel any ill will toward Luke because he knew that if the roles had been reversed, he would have done the same thing.

Jesse did his best to take the news in stride. More than that, he saw it was an opportunity to push himself. Freed from the Sammy sound, and the worlds of indie and alternative rock, he could get big and weird, turning from early Lou Reed to mid-seventies Bowie and Eno for inspiration. He could also go from writing about characters to creating one for himself. "It was like a new movie was starting." The idea for Laptop was being born. And because he didn't have a full-time job, and the offers to play overseas were still there, Jesse decided to push on. Sammy would continue, at least for a bit. When Jesse brought it up to Luke—one last tour—Luke wasn't interested. "I knew the record was dead in Europe," he says. "And I didn't want to go and play for seventy-plus people in Nottingham." Not content to just sit out the dates, and astute as always to the business side of things, Luke got himself legally removed from the band. This way, if the Sammy tour bus ran over a group of schoolkids in Gothenburg, Luke wouldn't be held responsible. Michael Galinsky once again was along on bass, while on drums they drafted in Belgian musician and graphic designer Herman Houbrechts, who played in a group called Nemo. To play Luke's parts Jesse drafted in their old college friend Ben Wheelock, who'd briefly played in their Wesleyan band Worrying Thing. Wheelock and Jesse had remained close over the years, and Luke would occasionally send Ben packages of Geffen CDs. Wheelock went through the set list, figuring out what to do on each song. "On a lot of the songs, I did simply learn the part," he says. "But there were times where I heard something I could add in that was different, and Jesse was completely open to it. We got along great throughout, with no disagreements or conflict."

Jesse in Europe on the final Sammy tour. Courtesy of Jesse Hartman.

The tour lasted a couple of weeks, taking in Belgium, Holland, Scandinavia, France, and Spain, places Sammy had never played. And despite the ominous clouds hanging over the future of the group, the vibe on the tour was positive. The musicians were having fun. "We'd play shows and make the songs sound however we could make them sound the best given who we were and what we had," says Wheelock. "It was a blast, and from the crowd response it felt like we totally pulled it off." Spain was the highlight. "We pulled into Valencia, and the DJ had named *Tales of Great Neck Glory* the Best Album of the Year," says Jesse. "So there were like three or four thousand kids at the show." It ended up being the biggest concert the band ever played as a headliner, and it led to a continuing love affair with Spain for Jesse.

Luke happened to be in Sweden trying to sign a group to DreamWorks when Sammy played Stockholm. He joined Sammy for a few songs (which made things awkward for his replacement; Wheelock had to leave the stage and hide in a small room, ducking down so he wouldn't be seen by the audience). It was fun, until it wasn't. "I didn't realize Ben was using a different tuning on the guitar than what I used to use," says Luke. He'd written his original parts using alternate tunings, and Wheelock had transposed them to standard tuning. This created havoc when Luke went to play his parts on Wheelock's guitar. Jesse, at first glad to have his old friend back by his side, glared at him. As Luke recalls, "I just thought, well, that's perfect Sammy." The whole night seemed to be cursed. The show was later shut down by Swedish cops; Jesse was never told what they had done wrong. "It was a fitting end, I think," he says. It was the last time Jesse and Luke would appear onstage together.

After the European tour, Sammy was done. They had no

SAMMY

label, Jesse was already brainstorming his next project, and Luke was focused full bore on his new duties at DreamWorks. It had been a fun ride, but it was over. Other than a couple of extra tracks from each of the album sessions, and a few tunes they'd recorded over the years in various places, there wasn't much in the archives. Sammy felt to them both like finished and settled business. Time to move on. When I ask the pair if there was ever a formal or official breakup announcement, a press release or something like that, both quicky answer, "No." After a second, Jesse adds, "No one cared."

3: WHATEVER HAPPENED TO YOUR OLD GUITAR?
DreamWorks, Laptop, Beats, and life after Sammy

Flying back from Sweden, Luke was thinking more about the band he didn't sign rather than anything having to do with Sammy. "I had moved on," he says. "I felt really proud that I'd had an opportunity to say something with music and do something with my friend." He didn't feel there was anything unresolved. He and Jesse had done the work and it was over. Luke's focus was now on DreamWorks and building something new. Although, for a while, he was going into his old office to do it. Because DreamWorks Records was distributed by Geffen, Luke was still reporting to the same building on Sunset. This was good and bad. Working right down the hall from his old space was not quite the clean break or fresh start he had envisioned. However, this allowed him some important continuity and closure, helping to shepherd a few projects he'd started at Geffen, such as records by Girls Against Boys and Phantom Planet. Within a year DreamWorks had its own space in Beverly Hills.

By now it was abundantly clear that the promise of grunge had petered out and there would be no more Nirvanas. Luke had seen it firsthand when Urge Overkill's *Saturation* had failed to connect. He began to think that maybe every great indie band shouldn't be on a major label. It was time to go back to basics and cultivate and nurture artists rather than chase the big and immediate bucks. Luke couldn't have been working with better people to make that happen. Lenny Waronker, who'd joined Warner Bros. as a junior A&R man in 1965, had a great ear and philosophy for playing the long game, investing in songwriters like Randy Newman and Van Dyke Parks. Joining him to run DreamWorks Records was Mo Ostin, another industry veteran (and legend) who had recently been running Warner Bros.

Luke's first big success was the emo band Jimmy Eat World, signing them after they'd been dropped by Capitol. Their debut for DreamWorks, *Bleed American*, released in 2001, helped the group score their biggest-ever hit with the LP's second single, "The Middle." Not content with just notching up huge sales, Luke also scored artistically, signing songwriter Elliott Smith. Luke had been a fan as far back as 1994 when he'd heard Smith's first solo record, *Roman Candle*, which had just been released on the tiny label Cavity Search.

Wanting to connect with the artist, Luke called all ten Steven Smiths he found in the Portland phone book (Elliott's first name at birth was Steven). This was when Smith was known primarily as being lead singer for the band Heatmiser. Every time someone picked up the phone, Luke would say, "Is this Elliott Smith from Heatmiser?" Finally, one of the voices tentatively answered, "Uh, yeah?" Luke just wanted to tell Smith his record was one of the greatest pieces of music he'd heard since *Nevermind*. Now, half a decade later, he was working with Smith at DreamWorks. While at the label, Smith released two heralded albums, *XO* and *Figure 8*, before his untimely death at thirty-four in October 2003.

Luke with Elliott Smith. Photo by Bootsy Holler.

One of the things that helped Luke become successful at A&R was his participation in Sammy. "Without Sammy, I would have never had the confidence to become an A&R person," he says. "It gave me a point of view and skill set I just did not have." Being in Sammy taught Luke what bands were up against. It taught him about stage design, lighting design, how merch works, how a publishing deal works. It allowed him to understand what it's like to be on tour and what sound check feels like, and it gave him exposure to the cadence of an artist's life. Knowledge he would put to good use when working with bands and performers.

Shortly after Elliott Smith died, DreamWorks was bought by Interscope. Luke had been through a few of these corporate shake-ups and mergers before, so he was used to the routine. The biggest change was that he was facing the prospect of working for Jimmy Iovine. Born in New York in 1953, Iovine began his career as a recording engineer, working out of the Record Plant and engineering albums for everyone from John Lennon to Meatloaf to Patti Smith. He cofounded Interscope Records in 1990. The label soon made a name for itself as a home for hip-hop, signing Tupac Shakur in 1991. Dr. Dre's massive album *The Chronic* followed a year later. At first, Luke was wary at the prospect of working with Iovine. Up to this point, he'd only known him as the competition. They'd fought over several bands (with Iovine, who had deeper pockets and a more storied history in the business, usually winning). The two met for breakfast to discuss Luke's possible future at Interscope.

The first thing Iovine asked Luke after they sat down was "What are you working on?" Luke played him something from one of his bands, AFI, and in a flash the two were in a deep discussion about the minutiae, and possibilities, of the song. Given his experience working on blockbuster LPs like *Born to Run* and *Damn the Torpedoes*, Iovine knew music inside and out, the technical and the emotional (as well as the business) aspects. He was the total package. "I fell in love with him in thirty seconds," Luke says. Seeing as how David Geffen had called Iovine prior to the meeting and vouched for Luke, the feeling was mutual. The only hitch was that, at the time, Interscope was the home of rap and a style of hard rock that Luke didn't care for. 50 Cent had just exploded and Eminem was huge, as was Marilyn Manson. "It was not really my culture," Luke says. But Iovine assured him that he wanted Luke's taste and voice at the label, so Luke stayed.

Luke and Iovine worked well together, and soon Luke became valuable at Interscope for another reason. As one of the few digital natives in the music business, Luke was always on the cutting edge of technology. More importantly, he saw the possibilities for the internet to help artists get fans and sell records. During this period, the music business was feeling the negative effects of Napster and file sharing—a new generation was beginning to see music as something that should be free—so Luke and Iovine found ways to develop corporate deals for artists (for example, Mary J. Blige having her own line of sunglasses). Luke eventually got so good at this he was made chief strategic officer in addition to being president of the label.

As part of the emerging paradigm of artists monetizing their fan engagement into non-musical artifacts, Iovine and Dr. Dre had the idea to make high-end headphones. Born Andre Romelle Young in Compton in 1965, Dr. Dre and his first group, World Class Wreckin' Cru, put out their debut in 1985. Even though his next project, N.W.A., was only active for a few years and released just two studio albums, they were extremely influential in launching the gangsta rap sound (their debut, *Straight Outta Compton*, is considered a classic of the genre). *The Chronic*, Dre's first solo record, ended up selling more than three million copies and won a Grammy for Best Rap Solo Performance. Iovine cofounded Beats in 2006 with Dre, and the first pair of headphones went on sale two years later. Beats had huge success right away thanks to endorsements by celebrities and athletes. In these early days, Beats was not a stand-alone company. The products were manufactured and distributed by Monster Cable Products. During this period, Luke's role in the company was minimal; he was only overseeing Universal's investment. However, he would soon be invited to join in a more official capacity.

SAMMY

The Beats crew: Jimmy Iovine, Dr. Dre, and Luke. Courtesy of Luke Wood.

The timing was good since Luke felt his career was at a crossroads. A critical point came when the explosive New York band Yeah Yeah Yeahs was in Silver Lake recording their third album for Interscope, *It's Blitz!* Luke loved the record, and he began to think like an A&R guy. What tracks could be singles? How could those songs be made more commercial? Coming up with answers to these questions was his job. "If you're on a major label, you're trying to have a hit," he says. "So how do we make it a hit? Is there anything more we could do?" As he sat there, listening to a playback of "Heads Will Roll," he thought about what would happen if the song crossed over and became a Top 40 hit. "It'll just drive more downloads," he recalls thinking. "It won't sell any more records." He scrapped the notes he'd been thinking of relaying to the group and just told them to release the record the way they wanted to. In that moment Luke realized the part of the job he loved—that dialogue with the artist, the back-and-forth to make the music even better than it already was—was no longer a thing; it didn't exist anymore. And yet, when Iovine called and invited him to come and help build Beats into a real company, Luke said no. Despite seeing the damage that downloading was doing to his industry and his company, Luke didn't want to abandon his artists. He considered working with musicians the greatest job in the world. Three months later, Iovine called again. Luke knew that if he turned him down, Iovine wouldn't ask a third time and so—wanting to take on the challenge of building something new—he took the job.

While Luke had been in Los Angeles concentrating on his new career at DreamWorks, Jesse was back in New York plotting his next move. Touring around Europe on the last Sammy tour in 1996, he'd heard a lot of music on the radio that he hadn't been hearing in the States, bands like Daft Punk, the robotic duo whose first LP, *Homework*, had just been released. "Things were getting more electronic," Jesse says, "and I was getting into it." It gave him the idea to add those elements and sounds into his own music. Almost a decade before LCD Soundsystem released a track about rock bands wanting to put down their guitars and get out synthesizers and samplers, that's just what Jesse did. It was an easy transition to make, seeing as how he'd never much been into the world of indie rock; Sammy had never toured with Sebadoh, and those groups were hardly his inspiration. Jesse saw it as his chance to push even further some of the seventies influences that had appeared around the margins of Sammy. "It's funny that Steve Shelley said the second record was too Bowie," Jesse says. "It wasn't Bowie enough for me."

Seeing as how he had a little money left from the Sammy

deal, he went to work recording new material. Whether these would end up being Sammy songs, or something else, Jesse didn't yet know. He just knew that it was going to sound different from what he'd been doing with Luke. Michael Corn, his old friend who'd played on Sammy's two LPs, was now working on music with a friend who lived in Westchester who had a sixteen-track reel-to-reel tape recorder in his parents' basement. The friend also had a sampler. In six months, they recorded five songs. On these new tunes, Jesse changed the way he sang. His voice was lower, and he was injecting more humor into his lyrics; he was playing a character. The songs, made from loops and samples in addition to live instruments, were also becoming cinematic. Listening to the tracks, Jesse realized, "This is not Sammy anymore. This is something completely different." He was invigorated by the new sound. But what was the next step? He didn't have a manager or a record deal. He was basically starting over.

Jesse turned to an old friend in the UK, David Barker. Barker had started Glass Records in the eighties before going on to work with both Fire and Creation. The timing for Jesse's call was perfect because Barker was just about to launch a new boutique label, God Bless Records. He put out the first Laptop record in 1997, an EP called *End Credits* made up of the five songs Jesse had made after the dissolution of Sammy. Even though not a lot of CDs were manufactured, Barker had a lot of contacts in the industry, so the right people heard it. The lead song, "End Credits," a humorous ode to breaking up with someone via their answering machine, became a minor hit in the UK. The only problem with all the attention brewing in England was that Jesse was back in New York. "Again, I'm in the wrong place at the wrong time." Not only that, but he didn't have a band, and those songs couldn't be played live anyway.

Two more songs appeared as singles, "Gimme the Nite" and "Whole Wide World." Both were popular and got radio play. This led to Jesse getting a call from Raymond Coffer, a big-time manager who had worked with Love and Rockets and Smashing Pumpkins. For once, Jesse could take the call. "The world was opening up to me in a way it hadn't with Sammy because no one could touch Sammy. For the first time, I was seeing what it was like to not have issues." Coffer also knew Luke and called him, asking about Jesse. Luke vouched for his old bandmate and told Coffer to work with him. Coffer was a larger-than-life character: brash, physically large, and with a shaved head. After Coffer traveled to New York, he and Jesse met with executives from all the major labels. These meetings proved so successful, they kicked off a bidding war. To seal the deal, Coffer set up a showcase gig at the Garage in London and invited all the competing labels. This was going to be the most important show of Jesse's life. But it wouldn't go off without a hitch.

The night before the gig, Jesse was given an address for the rehearsal space. When he got into a black cab, the driver—who, like all London cabbies, is supposed to have memorized thousands of streets in the densely laid-out capital—didn't know the address. He took Jesse to where he *thought* the street was. Jesse got out and wandered around for a bit with his guitar. It was getting late, and he was getting stressed. He came across a hospital with an ambulance parked out front. He stopped and asked the two ambulance drivers for directions. They couldn't have been more helpful. They spread out a map of London on the hood of the ambulance and showed Jesse how far off the mark he was. They also offered to give him a ride to the address. Opening the back of the ambulance, Jesse was startled to find a doctor and nurse in scrubs having tea. Seeing Jesse with his guitar, one of them remarked, "Oh, a pop star!" Jesse climbed in. The drivers put on the sirens and lights and proceeded to speed across the city in a mad scramble to get Jesse to the rehearsal space more or less on time.

The next day, the show went well. The CEO and head of A&R from Island Records came backstage after the performance. They offered him half a million dollars. "It was like a dream come true," says Jesse. "The best label, the most artist-friendly, and they made the biggest offer." There was just one problem. Universal Music Group was planning on buying PolyGram, who owned Island, and no one knew what was going to happen afterward. Jesse knew he might get screwed. Coffer advised Jesse to take the deal, so he did.

After Laptop signed to Island, Jesse considered moving to London to be closer to the label, but Coffer advised against this, telling Jesse he was unlikely to find any good musicians in the UK (a claim Jesse found laughable; weren't the Beatles from England? The Rolling Stones? Hundreds of other amazing groups and performers?). Flush with cash and seeing as how he was staying put in New York—and wanting to leave the various basements of the area behind him—Jesse set out to buy some new gear. He had a bit of luck, since Edward Douglas—the engineer who'd worked on *Tales of Great Neck Glory*—was now working at Sam Ash, the landmark music store in Midtown. Because Douglas had experience working with MIDI, samplers, synthesizers, and digital recording, he was assigned to the computer department. Douglas helped Jesse purchase $70,000 worth of computer gear, paid for by Island. It was everything they would need to set up a fully functioning recording studio within Jesse's apartment. Douglas then took a hiatus from Sam Ash and proceeded to work with Jesse on the next batch of Laptop songs.

Laptop promotional shot for Island Records. Courtesy of Jesse Hartman.

The first Laptop single for Island was "Nothing to Declare." Jesse codirected an elaborate green-screen video for the up-tempo electro track. Despite the label giving the song a big push, it wasn't as successful as the previous songs. As with Sammy, once Laptop got onto a major label, people didn't seem as interested in the project. Jesse was now just another major-label artist. To support the single, and begin to build up an audience for Laptop, Jesse put together a band of young musicians who played shows in Norway before touring with the electronic artist Les Rythmes Digitales on his UK dates. Edward Douglas came along on the tour to help with technical aspects, mostly overseeing the racks of gear that held the various triggered samples. Engineer Doug Henderson, who had been involved with recording and mixing "Nothing to Declare," came along as the house mixer. Although most of the tour went well, Jesse changed the set list for the Manchester show without informing Douglas, so when the band members started playing, the wrong sounds came out of the speakers, before Douglas realized what happened and quickly switched them to avoid anyone noticing.

Island did another single and video ahead of the planned full-length album. "I'm So Happy You Failed," a sort of spiritual sequel to Morrissey's "We Hate It When Our Friends Become Successful," is a buoyant and hilarious looks at schadenfreude. And even though it could be seen to allude to Sammy's troubles ("Word on the street says / Your second record's dead"), Jesse insists he wrote it about other bands he saw who were going through a difficult period. The video, a sort of mini–John Hughes flick with a huge cast of kids and adults playing teachers and students, was filmed in London with the set dressed up to be Jesse's old alma mater. At one point, he's fronting a band playing in a gymnasium to a group of kids sitting under a banner that says GREAT NECK HIGH, a sort of flashback to when his group the Sy's played for the entire school.

Right about when Jesse finished what he intended to be the first Laptop album, which he was calling *Guilt*, Universal finally took over Island. The executives who'd come backstage in London after the showcase were fired. Unlike a lot of other bands, Laptop wasn't immediately dropped, but *Guilt*'s release was in limbo and his new A&R rep didn't seem to get what Jesse was trying to do. Despite all this, Jesse tried to be optimistic. He wanted to give Universal a chance.

The new regime made an American deal with their affiliated label MCA to put out Laptop in the States. Wanting to be close to MCA, Jesse moved to Los Angeles, staying with Luke. The same as Sammy's song "Inland Empire," "I'm So Happy You Failed" came tantalizingly close to getting added to the big LA stations, but didn't quite make it. That's when Laptop was finally dropped from Island. As if that news wasn't bad enough, manager Raymond Coffer informed Jesse that he was also letting him go as a client. Luke, who by now knew how tough the music business could be, told his friend, "You're in the wrong line of work." Jesse was thirty, living in a city he didn't like, and he was once again faced with starting all over again. Looking back on "I'm So Happy You Failed," Jesse realizes how prophetic the track proved to be. "It ended up being about myself," he laughs, "although I didn't realize it at the time."

Once he started at Beats, Luke quickly discovered that his new job was insanely challenging and difficult. The record business had been simple: find a hit and then believe in and support the people who wrote the hit. Consumer electronics wasn't so simple. Luke had to manage massive global supply chains, sales and planning processes, forecasting, tariffs, battery compliance issues. Beats was also in more than eighty countries, with five hundred different wholesale accounts, a customer service division, and a global sales staff. It was not only a lot to deal with (to say the least), but there was also the added element of working with the press. As an A&R guy, Luke had preferred to be behind the scenes. He never took an executive producer credit on the records he worked on, and when it came to interviews, he let his artists do the talking. But headphones don't do interviews, and someone had to speak about the brand. Luke reluctantly took on the role, which was yet another skill he had to learn. It wasn't easy. In 2011 he was asked to speak at a supplier conference in Taiwan. He wasn't quite sure what it entailed, but he agreed. When he got there, he was led to the edge of a huge conference room that held six thousand people. One of the organizers asked Luke for the thumb drive that held his presentation. Stunned, Luke asked, "Presentation? I just thought I'd talk about Beats." He'd never made a Keynote or PowerPoint in his life, let alone delivered one. They told him he had thirty minutes, and that the crowd wanted pictures of the products and slides on brand history. Luke managed to muddle his way through, but it was the first of many lessons he'd receive.

Back in Los Angeles, as different variations of headphones were being developed, there were always two songs that Beats executives and engineers used to test and calibrate new models: "In da Club" by 50 Cent and "Refugee" by Tom Petty and the Heartbreakers. The two tracks obviously speak to the history and influences of the two cofounders: Dr. Dre coproduced the 50 Cent track, while Jimmy Iovine coproduced "Refugee." Dre and Iovine ended up hearing each song thousands of times during their years at the company. While Luke also logged repeated listens to that pair of tunes, he secretly added a third: "Say It Ain't So" from Weezer's debut. He chose the song because—like Dre's and Iovine's choices—he knew the track intimately. Luke was director of marketing for Geffen/DGC when Weezer had been in the studio, so he'd been invited down to watch them record. Knowing how the song was made, and what it felt like to hear it in a professional studio, made it useful for testing the EQ, compression, imaging, and depth of the various Beats models. Besides, as Luke says, "I love that song, so I did not mind listening to it literally fifty thousand times."

As the company grew, Beats eventually moved into a 200,000-square-foot office in Culver City. The spacious and colorful space, designed by Bestor Architecture, boasted features such as a café, gym, and several communal working spaces (in addition to the usual office-building staples of conference rooms, private offices, and a reception area). The company launched Beats Music, a subscription-based streaming service, in 2014. Beats was sold to Apple later that same year for $3 billion, an amazing achievement considering the company had been around for less than a decade.

As if changing careers and helping to make Beats a success wasn't enough to keep him busy, during these years Luke married his college sweetheart and started a family. He met Sophia Nardin in September of 1990, when they were both starting their senior year at Wesleyan. They got married a decade later at a small, private ceremony in Hawaii. They have two kids, daughters Ella, born in 2000, and Georgia, who came along in 2003.

That Luke was seeing such success was not a surprise to anyone who knew him. "The first time I ever met Luke," recalls college friend and his temporary replacement in Sammy, Ben Wheelock, "I could tell that he was bound to excel in whatever road he chose, which was most likely going to be music-related." Another college friend, Cynthia Nelson, who'd played in the Wesleyan band Worrying Thing, told me something very similar. "You could kind of tell that whatever Luke did, he was going to be successful, at least in terms of working hard and being unafraid to do whatever needs to be done and working outside the box." Hugh Flynn, Luke's bandmate from his very first group, Nehru Zombie, could see these qualities as the two were coming of age in Rochester. "Luke is a force of nature and always has been," Flynn says. "While I wouldn't have been able to guess exactly how he'd find that success, massive success was always the only possible option for him. He's a smart man with vision. That's a good combination." Remembers musician Rebecca Odes, "Luke has a brilliant business mind, and has always been absolutely attuned to that part of himself—a real rarity for a person who also has strong creative sensibilities. His career trajectory makes total sense to me."

Apple buying Beats wasn't the only big purchase in Luke's life that year. In 2014, he bought the historic mid-century modern home known as Silvertop. The house, which sits on a hill overlooking the Silver Lake reservoir, had been commissioned by industrialist Kenneth Reiner in 1956. Reiner hired famed architect John Lautner to build it. The result was a stunning structure featuring concrete curves and futuristic touches that has since been heralded as a classic (a frequent location for film and television, in 2025 it provided the backdrop for the second episode of the first series of Seth Rogen's Hollywood satire *The Studio*). When it came on the market (for only the second time), Luke and his family were living just a few streets away; he hadn't moved from the neighborhood since arriving in 1994. The house cost $8 million. To renovate the home, Luke hired Bestor Architecture, the firm that had worked on the Beats headquarters in Culver City. Renovations ended up taking three years and cost almost as much as the house itself, but it was all worth it. Silvertop continues to be a dazzling architectural marvel, at once both classic and forward-looking.

Part of the home includes a state-of-the-art recording studio, a space where Luke spends considerable time. Despite Sammy being inactive, making music has continued to be a big part of his life. Even now, Luke spends as much as an hour a day playing guitar. He's also been writing songs with former Creeper Lagoon singer Ian Sefchick (Luke signed Creeper Lagoon to DreamWorks back in 2000). Another way Luke's stayed close to the musical world is by joining Fender's board of directors. He did so at the request of his friends Bono and the Edge, who joined at the same time (the Irish superstars figured they might miss a few board meetings, and they wanted someone on the inside who could report back with details). Luke's work on the board consists of helping to formulate the privately held company's long-term strategic planning, something Luke calls "a tremendous honor."

Never one to sit still for long, in 2023 Luke opened Jellyman Tea, a new business serving boba, coffee, and milk tea located in the Sunset Junction area of Silver Lake (it's basically the hippest part of the hip enclave). Jellyman is a partnership with award-winning actor, rapper, writer, and director Donald Glover, a.k.a. Childish Gambino. Luke got a taste for boba during his various travels throughout Southeast Asia, including trips to Taipei, where boba is from. He met Glover during COVID, and the two came up with the idea for Jellyman to explore ideas around storytelling and world-building within the food and beverage industry. One of Jellyman's inspired offerings is the Peanut Butter and Jelly, Man, which is made with grape jelly, peanut milk, and maple sea salt foam. The space was designed once again by Bestor Architecture, and Luke can often be found there enjoying some boba.

Luke as he looks today. Courtesy of Luke Wood.

Over the years, Luke and Jesse have stayed close, talking on the phone, and occasionally meeting up. Before COVID, they even got together and recorded a new Sammy song. Lately, Luke's been devoting time to his next venture, which has to do with sneakers and will launch soon.

When I ask him where his drive comes from, Luke answers quickly. "It comes from when we were abandoned when I was eighteen months old. My mother bonded very deeply with me. And once she had to leave and go to the workforce full-time, I felt abandoned by her. And I'm always trying to get away from that feeling of being alone.

I'm always running forward. I'm always fleeing." This is why Luke's comfortable in the uncomfortable. He needs to constantly find and immerse himself in new things, venture into fields and industries he knows nothing about, start his own companies, learn—and conquer—new areas. "I always thought I could achieve things higher than maybe other people thought I could achieve," he says. "I just always had this high aspiration for myself that wasn't always articulated with who I was in the world. It's not a narcissism, it's just a belief, like *I can do this*." He's proven repeatedly that he can.

On one of Laptop's tours of Europe, Jesse met and became friendly with Norwegian DJ Marit Karlsen. Like David Barker a few years prior, Karlsen had been wanting to start a record label. This worked out well for Jesse, seeing as how he was sitting on a lot of unreleased Laptop material. And whereas other prospective labels hadn't been able to extricate him from his Universal contract, Karlsen managed to secure Laptop's release. This left Jesse free to sign to the newly formed Trust Me Records. Rather than release *Guilt*, the same LP Jesse had ready to go for Island, he broke apart the record, adding new tracks and scattering the others over what would eventually be two albums: 2000's *Opening Credits* and 2001's *The Old Me vs. the New You*.

The records received raves on both sides of the Atlantic. *Melody Maker*, in a four-star review for *Opening Credits*, called it "a bona fide mini-classic." The *NME* praised *The Old Me* and declared "rarely has the sound of going nowhere fast been so satisfying." Tony Fletcher in *New York Newsday* wrote that "Hartman is heartless, but he's also hilarious," and Jesse even made the cover of *CMJ* magazine, his glowering

SAMMY

face floating above the headline HE'S SO HAPPY YOU FAILED. (Later in the year he would tell the *New York Press*, "It was the most anonymous cover of *CMJ* in history. I didn't get a single call from anyone telling me they had seen it.") Not only was Jesse, along with the new records, receiving accolades, but it seemed that past sins were also absolved: "One-man band Jesse Hartman was a member of Pavement tribute band Sammy," wrote *Alternative Press*, "but, hey, all is forgiven now."

During his stay in Los Angeles, before the Island deal went south, Luke had helped Jesse get a job at an internet start-up called musician.com. A partnership with Guitar Center, it was run by several record label executives who were trying to make the switch to the newly booming internet era. The site combined content with the idea to sell musical gear to musicians. Jesse was a product director, coming up with ideas for content for the site. It was a good gig, allowing him to travel to conferences and meetings in various cities. He even convinced the company to open a New York studio where he could interview artists and have musicians perform. This allowed him to travel back and forth to New York. On one of his trips, he went with a friend to a book party at Sebastian Junger's bar in Chelsea the Half King. Jesse had just been given finished copies of *Opening Credits* and, even though the literary crowd wasn't his scene, he wanted to show his CD to a writer friend he knew who would be at the gathering. At the party, he met literary agent Emilie Stewart. Jesse was instantly smitten and, with her in New York and not much keeping him in Los Angeles, he moved back to Manhattan. For a while he lived in the musician.com studio, which was in a building in the East Village his brother owned. It didn't last long. The website, and his job, both got swept away when the internet bubble burst in 2000.

Jesse and Emilie got married in 2002 at the New York Aquarium, a sentimental choice seeing as how his parents met on the beach at Coney Island in 1950. Luke attended and was one of the four guests holding up a chuppah pole. Jesse wrote a song for his vows and then sang it and played guitar during the ceremony. The wedding band was an instrumental jazz-funk group from Harlem called Stuff who'd been signed to Warner Bros. Records in the seventies. R&B singer Gary U. S. Bonds joined as a guest, and even though both the band and Bonds didn't start performing until late in the evening, when they finally did, it was worth it.

The following year, Laptop's third record, *Don't Try This at Home*, was released on yet another new label, Gammon. To promote the record, Jesse put together an all-female band, which included Emilie on keyboards. Jesse also wrote a screenplay to go along with the album.

Once the tour and promotional cycle for *Don't Try This at Home* was over, Jesse turned to a dream he'd had for a long time: to open a restaurant with his brother. Jesse and Phil got some investors and bought a building in the East Village. Jesse then spent years working with architects and engineers in addition to chasing down permits and dealing with banks. It was a complicated, and expensive, project. Built on the site of a former fabric warehouse and brothel, in the summer of 2005 Jesse and Phil opened a two-story restaurant called Mo Pitkin's House of Satisfaction (the name was supposedly inspired by an eccentric cousin who'd tried to assassinate Hitler). Boasting a full kitchen serving "Judeo-Latino" cuisine in addition to two bars and two stages, Jesse told *The Village Voice* he wanted the venue to be "Part Max's Kansas City, part Second Avenue Deli, and part Mercer Arts Center." It was a heady and hectic period; Emilie, five months pregnant, tended bar.

As soon as it opened, the restaurant was a huge success and quickly proved to be a magnet for artists and celebrities. Always packed, everyone from Lin Manuel-Miranda to Moby would stop by. The venue hosted nightly performances of music, burlesque, and comedy shows with names like "Chicks and Giggles" and "I Eat Pandas." Jesse was having a blast, and yet he was torn. In 2006 his son Charlie was born, and he wanted to be home for that. At the same time, at the restaurant he was Humphrey Bogart in *Casablanca*, posing for pictures with celebrities and being at the center of a cool new scene that he'd created from scratch. None of it left much space for music.

He ended up rewriting the screenplay for *Don't Try This at Home* and turned it into *House of Satisfaction*, a film that uses the restaurant as a main location. Jesse directed the movie and stars in it. It's a fun watch, especially for Sammy fans since his character, Jesse Limbo, sings a few Sammy songs in the movie, including an end-credit duet of "Babe Come Down" with Luna's Britta Phillips, who plays his ex-wife in the movie. Ironically, the movie never got much distribution due to issues around the music—Jesse's own music, which he did not have the rights to.

Despite the popularity and the crowds, Mo Pitkin's House of Satisfaction closed in 2007. The restaurant was too expensive to keep going, and the brothers simply ran out of money. "It was a lot of fun," Jesse says, "but the restaurant business is super tough." They managed to sell the building right before the real estate crash of 2008. While that turned out to be a lucky break, Jesse was once again left to try and figure out his next move. The restaurant had taken a lot out of him, plus he was saddled with a huge amount of credit card debt. He also had a precocious two-year-old at home. "That was not a time to make a fourth album," he says.

Jesse toyed with the idea of starting a new restaurant, and he also pitched a few film ideas to MTV. What he settled on was building a business around the talented cinematographers he'd met working on his movie. With the crew he'd assembled, they could create branded content and shoot commercials. Jesse would do the editing. The business took off quickly. His wife also got involved when it was too much for just Jesse to deal with. At one point they had a big office in Manhattan with fifteen employees. They've since scaled back to make it more manageable. During this period, their daughter, Marlena (she goes by Lulu) was born.

As their son Charlie grew up, Jesse and Emilie were not finding a good fit for him at any of the local schools. When he was in the third grade, they finally transferred Charlie to a school for gifted kids on Long Island. It was a trek getting there every day from their apartment in Lower Manhattan, so they decided to buy a home in the area. Jesse didn't want to necessarily move back to Long Island, but in 2015 they bought a house in Cold Spring Harbor, a town about thirty minutes from where he grew up in Great Neck.

A few years ago, they took a family trip to Nevis in the Caribbean. There were a bunch of musicians hanging out at the hotel bar, some of whom were visiting while others were local. Among them was Michael Desmarais, an English drummer who'd been in the Winkies, a band who'd put out a self-titled album on Chrysalis in 1975. Desmarais later worked with John Cale and Brian Eno. Even though

Desmarais was twenty years older than Jesse, the two hit it off, and by the end of the week they were jamming at the hotel. A few months later, during a trip to Valencia in Spain—a city Jesse has loved ever since it gave a warm welcome to Sammy back in 1996— Jesse once again ran into Desmarais, who was there with his wife. Jesse and Desmarais, aided by some local musicians, met in a studio and laid down a bunch of tracks. Kids Charlie and Lulu joined in, singing on several tunes.

Laptop 2.0: Charlie and Jesse Hartman. Photo by David Nicholas.

The following summer, they all did the same thing. More recording, more songs. After the two sessions, Jesse found he was sitting on seventy tunes. Not only that, but the material was strong; this wasn't just noodling around or holiday jamming. He decided it was time to reboot his Laptop. And just to bring everything completely full circle, Edward Douglas—the engineer on *Kings of the Inland Empire* and *Tales of Great Neck Glory*—mixed some of the songs.

This time around, Jesse didn't want Laptop to be another

one-man band; he's relaunched the project as a father-son duo. Charlie appears alongside Jesse in the press photos and features prominently in the band's videos (which are once again directed by Jesse). Laptop even played its first shows in decades in England during the summer of 2025, and new singles and videos will continue to appear in the lead-up to the fourth Laptop record, *On This Planet*.

For a recording project that was built on a foundation of bachelor-hedonism and wry swipes at ex-girlfriends, it's ironic and kind of wonderful that Laptop features Charlie, the product of a long and happy marriage. It's not an ending, or a new beginning (depending on how you look at it), that anyone could have seen coming. Nearly twenty-five years ago, Simon Price wrote in *The Independent*, "In Laptop's world, there are no happy ever-afters, only the gallows' humor of the serially heartbroken." When I see video on Instagram of Jesse standing on a London stage alongside his son, smiling and playing new songs, it certainly seems like a happy ever after to me.

For a band who only released two records and an EP, and only lasted for a couple of years, the cast of characters who played a part in the Sammy story is surprisingly large. Where they've all ended up is just as compelling as the journeys Jesse and Luke have taken that have led them to where they are today.

By 2007, Sammy and Laptop engineer Edward Douglas had mostly moved out of the music world, working as a film critic and reviewing movies for several publications. Since 2001, he also has written his own weekly newsletter dedicated to movies called *The Weekend Warrior*.

SAMMY

Girls Against Boys drummer Alexis Fleisig, who played on *Tales of Great Neck Glory* and Laptop's *Don't Try This at Home*, has continued to play with GVSB during various incarnations and reunions. He also formed the band Paramount Styles with GVSB member Scott McCloud. In addition to his work as a musician, Fleisig is a renowned graphic designer, photographer, and filmmaker, shooting music videos for Sub Pop and other record labels.

Rebecca Odes, who played bass during Sammy's trip to England in 1994 and on their appearance on *The Jon Stewart Show*, released a single and an EP as Odes. She also cofounded the website gurl.com in 1996, and in 2013 she founded wifey.tv, an internet-based platform for women. In 2024, label 12XU released a two-vinyl Love Child collection entitled *Never Meant to Be 1988–1993*. In addition to her work as a musician, Odes is a writer and visual artist. She splits her time between California and New York.

Brendan O'Malley, who drummed alongside Odes on UK and US TV appearances, as well as playing on two songs on *Tales of Great Neck Glory*, has largely retreated from music to focus on his career in academia. After getting his PhD in history from the City University of New York, he has taught history at the college level at many area schools.

In 1996, when it seemed that every big label in the UK needed to have an indie band, Billy Reeves, Sammy's PR rep at Fire Records, looked at the charts and thought, "I could do that." Reeves was so confident, he made a hundred-pound bet with an art director at *Melody Maker* that, within a year, he would form a band, sign to a major label, and have a hit. And that's exactly what he did. Reeves formed Theaudience with Sophie Ellis-Bextor, the daughter of a TV star, and signed to Mercury Records. Reeves chalks up his success to Sammy. "I bought the house I'm sitting in now because of Luke and Jesse teaching me how to write songs and how to run a band," he says. "That week of Sammy led to me signing a massive deal and getting in the charts, and it all started with those guys." In 2001, Reeves was in a near-fatal car accident that landed him in the hospital for four months. He eventually went back to school and got a post-graduate degree in broadcasting. Reeves now works at the BBC and is releasing music under his own name; his most recent record—2024's *When Lord God Almighty Reads the News*—contains a cover of the Laptop tune "Let's Not." He and Jesse are still friends.

After breaking up in 1997, That Dog—featuring *Kings of the Inland Empire* drummer Tony Maxwell—reunited in 2011. In 2019 they released their fourth album, *Old LP.* Original drummer Maya Rudolph returned to sing background vocals. In addition to his work in That Dog, Maxwell has worked as a composer and music supervisor for feature films *Chuck & Buck* and *The Good Girl*, as well as overseeing creative marketing efforts at VH1 and Nickelodeon.

Smells Like Records founder Steve Shelley continued to drum for Sonic Youth until the group broke up in 2011. He's also played alongside numerous musicians live and on record over the years, including Sun Kil Moon, Mark Eitzel, and M. Ward. Smells Like ceased operations years ago, but Shelley has resurrected some of its catalog as part of a new label called Vampire Blues.

Jesse's childhood friend Michael Corn—who played on more Sammy songs than anyone besides Jesse or Luke—has remained active in music for the past thirty years. In addition to scoring movies and TV shows like *Pawn Stars* and *Wahlburgers*, Corn was in the band Heydevils and he formed a duo with Cliff Mays called Mays & Corn. The duo also performs in Grateful BRO, a popular Westchester, New York–based classic rock and Dead band. In his latest musical project, Autorub, Corn plays all the instruments and sings. Much of Autorub's songs are political satire.

Drummer Tim Orr turned from rock to jazz and roots music projects after playing in Jesse and Luke's college band Worrying Thing. He also acted as the associate director of the Brubeck Institute, and he's written about drumming for a number of publications. Today, he plays in multiple bands in and around the San Francisco area, and he does marketing, PR, and archival work for the Monterey Jazz Festival.

After teaching himself Photoshop, Ben Wheelock, who played guitar in Sammy and Laptop, and bass in Worrying Thing, went on to have a career in graphic design, working primarily in the music industry. During his tenure at TVT Records in the late nineties, he created striking sleeves for the Guided by Voices albums *Do the Collapse* and *Isolation Drills*. He still writes and plays music, but is not currently in a band, though he's working on a new musical project.

Cynthia Nelson, who played bass in Worrying Thing, has had a long career in music since the nineties. She played in Ruby Falls as well as Retsin alongside Rodan's Tara Jane O'Neil. Her latest group is the Cynthia Nelson Band. She also starred in the 1994 indie rock film *Half-Cocked*, which was cowritten by Michael Galinsky, who played bass in both Sammy and Laptop.

Jesse's brother Phil continues to operate popular restaurants in the New York area. Two Boots Pizza has become a Manhattan mainstay, with its original location on

Avenue A still open. For several years, Phil ran the business alongside his son, Leon. Leon is currently a filmmaker in Los Angeles, and Phil is also writing a book about his experiences.

Worrying Thing's bassist John Steeb passed away of a drug overdose in 2004 at the age of thirty-six. Dave Ford, the drummer who played in an early version of Worrying Thing, as well as in Luke's high school band Nehru Zombie, has also passed away. After getting a degree in film from SUNY Purchase, Ford worked in the film industry and later taught classes in cinematography and lighting. He died in Rochester in 2018 at the age of fifty-one.

In college, Nehru Zombie bassist Hugh Flynn became more focused on his undergraduate degree in physics than being in a group, and for decades after he didn't pick up an instrument. "I thought the band experience was a great, amazing, and fun thing to have done," he says, "but Luke really had a vision for something bigger. That was just never a place I was interested in heading." In his forties, Hugh started taking guitar lessons over Zoom, and these days he plays out in local bands around Boston, where he lives. In addition, he has a son in high school, also named Hugh, who shares his passion for playing music. The same spark that Hugh discovered alongside Luke all those years ago has been passed on to a new generation. "I now get to enjoy going out to see my son play with his band," he says, "and that's kind of magical."

Jesse knows the feeling. His son, Charlie—in addition to appearing alongside him in Laptop—attends Wesleyan and is starting to write his own songs. And not only is Charlie grappling with many of the same choices and opportunities that Jesse had at his age, but he looks just like him. Where should Charlie go from here? What does his future hold?

Life is finite, and when we select one path over another, we set a course for our life to follow. Sometimes we can change that course, backtrack, and set off on a different direction. Sometimes we can't. Sometimes we realize too late that the path we're following is the wrong one. For Sammy, the choices were stark and almost immediate: Is the band everything, or isn't it? Were Jesse and Luke going to devote their entire lives to making it work—eating, drinking, and sleeping Sammy—or was the band just something they were doing for fun, a way to spend time together as friends? Jesse's parents had been devastated when he took that break in college to tour with Richard Hell; his mom had literally wept. So, for him, becoming a full-time musician was not going to happen. "Even though my family is so art-focused, there was always a feeling like, you had to do something real," says Jesse. "You had to have a backup plan. You couldn't just be a full-time artist." There was also no safety net. The parents who'd given Jesse and Luke good lives were not handing out huge inheritances, and there were no cushy family businesses they were being groomed to one day take over. If they were going to have financial stability of any sort, they would need to make it happen by themselves. "If I didn't make money, I didn't have money," says Luke. "So the idea of being a musician seemed like a suicide run into poverty."

The indie and alternative scenes found a lot of groups operating at one end of two economic extremes. On one side you had trust fund kids, like the Strokes, who came from privileged backgrounds and were going to be rich no matter what. On the other side were groups who had nothing to lose, like Nirvana, lower-middle-class types with no college education and no real prospects (Kurt Cobain's dad worked in a gas station when he was born, and Kurt himself had worked as a janitor). Sammy was stuck right in the middle. Sure, Jesse and Luke were raised on the higher end of middle class, but they always worked, always had jobs. They were each like Nick Carraway, living in the shadow of Jay Gatsby's gigantic mansion—always on the outside looking in. The band's attitude, says Luke, was "Let's make music, but we're not going to quit everything else we want to do in our lives unless we really think it's going to go to a place that has a much bigger platform and a much bigger audience." Jesse concurs, and then adds, "But there's a kind of chicken-and-egg thing here, where sometimes you have to dive in to know. We dove in in our own way, but we didn't dive in as much as some of the other bands were diving in."

The fact that there were only two members in Sammy meant they had to be in lockstep when it came to decisions, including the most important one of all. "It was like on *Seinfeld*," says Jesse. "We had a pact. There was an understanding that the band really wasn't going to be the thing unless both people looked each other in the eye and said, 'This is what we have to do now.' And I don't think I would have wanted to do that if Luke wasn't fully ready to go." That moment never arrived for either of them. Jesse had a lot going on in New York. Film projects, his family, his brother's restaurants. His identity was Lou Reed and Woody Allen. He wanted to stay in New York. Luke, meanwhile, was not only loving his life in Los Angeles, but he was excelling beyond any sort of expectations he could have ever had for himself. Was he going to give all of that up, and risk the financial well-being of his wife and kids, just to play out some rock-and-roll fantasy? Sure, as a kid he'd jumped around in front of a mirror with a tennis racket, pretending to be in Blondie, but he wasn't a kid anymore. And yet, when I ask Luke if there could have been some situation that would have been enticing enough for him to leave his job, he answers, "There was definitely a scenario where that would have happened." Jesse agrees. "I guess if things had just skyrocketed beyond belief, it could have forced the hand," he says. "But otherwise, it was always going to remain what it kind of started out being."

When having discussions about anything to do with Sammy, I always spoke to Jesse and Luke together. I wanted to do this to make sure we were all on the same page in terms of memories and facts. I didn't want to play a game of back-and-forth with the group's history, nor did I want to descend into backbiting and score-settling, being sold self-serving memories (*Rashomon*'s a good movie, but I didn't want to enter that forest). Another thing I wanted was to see Jesse and Luke together, even if we were just all on video. How did they act in each other's company? Were there smiles? Was there any trace of bitterness or acrimony? Was the friendship still there?

We often idolize if not idealize bands. We see them as tight-knit gangs, inseparable units, blood-brother partnerships forged on the road through months and years of trials and tribulations. But often the reality's something much drier and transactional: bands can be a business, a deal, merely a contract. Whether it's the Ramones, Oasis, or Simon & Garfunkel, there have been plenty of groups who were no longer friends or even friendly toward each other, onstage or off. Sammy, I quickly discovered, was not one of those groups. During our conversations, it was fun to see Jesse and Luke together, laughing as they tried to remember who played bass at Jack's Sugar Shack, or recounting how their records were made. It became apparent to me that, while I'd set out to write a book about a band, what I ended up spending most of my time documenting was a friendship. After all, Sammy lasted about three years, but Jesse and Luke have been friends for ten times that. The key to that lasting friendship is that they're complementary in the truest sense of the word. Jesse had never met anyone like Luke, and Luke had never met anyone like Jesse. As Billy Reeves says to me, "Their relationship was really interesting. It was almost like they wanted to be each other."

I think of this a few weeks later when Luke writes an email to me and Jesse, "I always think of Sammy as Huck Finn and Tom Sawyer." When we're introduced to Huckleberry Finn early in *The Adventures of Tom Sawyer*, we keenly feel the admiration and awe that Sawyer has for the outcast. As Twain writes, "Tom was like the rest of the respectable boys in that he envied Huckleberry . . ." And why not? Huck Finn didn't have to go to school or church, and he slept whenever (and wherever) he chose. If he wanted to go swimming, he did, and he didn't have to concoct (and not get away with) an elaborate alibi the way Tom did. But as the son of the town drunk, shunned and "cordially hated" by all the town's mothers, Huck must have envied the stability, safety, and love that Tom had. When Huck and Tom and a boy named Joe Harper are presumed dead in a drowning accident, only for the trio to reappear at their own funeral days later, there are tears of joy for the resurrected Tom and Joe, but no one's glad to see Huck. Tom has a home and relatives who miss him. Huck has nothing. They're drawn to each other because each one has something the other lacks or desires.

Together, Jesse and Luke—like Huck and Tom—had grand adventures, pushed boundaries, learned lessons, and discovered things about themselves along the way. They built a metaphorical raft and went on a journey. "We started floating down this river meeting these characters Jesse invented, or repurposed," writes Luke, "and we built a Sammy world." But all rivers empty into the ocean eventually, and all adventures turn into something else. "The answer to why Sammy perhaps ended has nothing to do with what label we were on, what the reviews said, did we still sound like Pavement, my new A&R career . . . perhaps it's as simple as the raft full of these characters ran into the sea, we learned who we were in the process, and it was time to build new worlds."

My final joint conversation with Jesse and Luke takes place over Zoom in September. We start speaking at eleven in the morning, West Coast time. As the conversation begins to wind down (me reaching the end of my questions, and the guys reaching the end of their patience for my endless questions), I ask them how they feel about Sammy. Do they view it as an adventure, an asterisk, a missed opportunity? Jesse takes a long pause before answering. "I put it out of my mind a little bit, and it's been fun to revisit," he finally replies. "I kind of love it. I kind of hate it sometimes. But it was a very important period of time, and in retrospect it seems like a very powerful time. I don't really have any regrets about it." Luke agrees, reflecting on the end of the band, "We were never really that sad. It was a very funny ride. We did this thing out of love for each other, and a love for a certain kind of music."

For Jesse, if there's a downside, it's in not knowing what could have or might have happened with the group. "All the bands that I grew up listening to always had like three or four albums to kind of figure it out. And we didn't really have that, which is a little sad." But he then adds, "Had I not met Luke, maybe nobody would have ever heard *anything*. Because most of the people I knew in New York didn't come close to getting the attention we got in those few years."

Luke's only ever had one moment of remorse or sadness in terms of what didn't happen for Sammy. It happened when he went to New York to meet with the Strokes to try and get them to sign to DreamWorks. "I honestly thought they accomplished what we wanted to on *Tales of Great Neck Glory*. They just did it better." He has a point. The Strokes combined all that Television/Modern Lovers/Velvet Underground mojo that Sammy had captured on numerous tracks and turned it into world-dominating zeitgeist. The Strokes even copped some of Sammy's look. But Luke is quick to add, "I'm not saying they ripped us off in any way, shape, or form. If you asked them, they probably never even heard of Sammy. But I'm just saying, to me, when I saw them, I was like, *Oh, shit, if we'd done a few things differently, that was a path for us. We could have been that band*. And I would have loved to have been in that band."

Jesse has a similar story. When he was performing as Laptop, in London, at a hotel bar, and the Strokes were in the UK on their first tour. "I'd already moved on and I was doing something different, but I couldn't believe how much of a prototype we had been for that. And that was not our Pavement side." Despite our earlier conversation about the California band, where Jesse and Luke had just brushed it aside, mostly making light of the situation, it's clear how deeply those early comparisons hurt and dampened the trajectory of Sammy. "Whoever wrote the first article about the Pavement thing, it's like every other journalist just copied and pasted something from that point forward," Jesse says. "And I felt that nobody was really listening to where the thing was headed."

We all pause. This seems like a good place, if not a depressing one, to end. We've been on the call for hours and I feel I need to let these guys go. It's a Friday and getting late on the East Coast. Jesse's daughter should be home from school by now. The weekend's almost here. Dinner might need to be prepared, and I might be keeping him from it. But I can tell that Jesse doesn't want to end on a down note. And as if to remind himself, and to impress upon me, that there are no hard feelings and that—for the most part—Sammy was a good and positive experience, he has one last story to tell this history hound.

When they were in Northern California to play Live 105's BFD festival, as part of the tour for *Great Neck Glory*, they were hanging out in the bar after they played with Aaron Axelsen. A lifelong music fan, Axelsen had started in college radio, worked in record stores, and got an internship before getting hired full-time at Live 105 in 1996. He was known for championing small bands and breaking groups (he would later be the first DJ in the US to play "Mr. Brightside" by the Killers). At the time, the Sammy single "Neptune Ave." was getting about twenty-five plays a week on Axelsen's station. A respectable number which hinted that it was close to getting added to the full rotation. Luke knew Axelsen well from his job at Geffen, which meant he knew that Axelsen was a fanatic basketball fan who also played the sport. Luke similarly knew that Jesse had been on the varsity high school basketball team back in Great Neck, and he'd witnessed his bandmate's skills firsthand during a couple of pickup games in New York when they'd played alongside Phil Hartman. So Luke came up with a bet: Jesse would play Aaron in a game of one-on-one, and if Jesse won, "Neptune Ave." would get added to Live 105's full rotation. (Neither Jesse nor Luke can remember what they bet against this in the event they lost.) Aaron was willing, and cocky, repeatedly boasting how good he was. No one could beat him. He could sink three-pointers. This was going to be a cakewalk. So, in the middle of the night, they found a park in a nearby neighborhood and procured a basketball. The game was on.

Seeing as how it was summer, Aaron was ready to go wearing long, baggy, nineties shorts along with a large black T-shirt and a black backward baseball cap. Jesse, meanwhile, disappeared for a quick costume change. When he reappeared, he was decked out in New Balance sneakers, running shorts, and a purple-and-yellow LA Lakers basketball jersey that practically glowed in the dark. A few days earlier—just for the hell of it—Sammy had stopped at a sporting goods store in Orange County, where they all bought matching basketball uniforms to wear during a concert. Seemed like a funny idea in the moment. Now, a few days later, Jesse was called upon to don the uniform again.

Michael Corn, Jesse's childhood friend who played drums on the tour, was there and took pictures of the match. In the photos, Aaron's grinning wildly and looking confident. Jesse, even though much alcohol had been consumed prior to this, has a face filled with a smile but also a grim determination.

SAMMY

You can tell that it's late because beyond a chain-link fence bordering the court there's a large apartment building, and every window is dark.

Even though he hadn't played basketball seriously in five or six years, Jesse quickly dominated. He made basket after basket, scored point upon point. "It was like a supernatural moment," he remembers. "Like lifting the car off your kid. It was just one of those things where, to get that airplay, I was like Steph Curry." It wasn't even close; Jesse smoked Aaron. "Jesse couldn't miss," agrees Luke. "It was insane."

When I ask if the bet was honored, and if the increased rotation of Sammy's song ended up helping at all, both Jesse and Luke laugh and say no. "It backfired," adds Jesse. "Like many things in Sammy." Maybe so, but for a band who had played ironically with the ideas of being kings, creating empires, and achieving glory, and who drew sharp character studies of lovable losers, that night they won. "It was a glorious moment," declares Jesse. "It was everything that Sammy was meant to be."

"That's exactly right," Luke says. "We went for the shot."

END CREDITS

First and foremost, I want to thank Jesse Hartman and Luke Wood for their generosity in sharing with me their time and memories. This book obviously could not have been written without their cooperation, and they were each friendly, open, and helpful all along the way. I also want to thank everyone who spoke to me directly or who responded to interview questions via email: Michael Corn, Dennis Dennehy, Edward Douglas, Larry Fessenden, Alexis Fleisig, Hugh Flynn, Phil Hartman, Marcelo Krasilcic, Louie Max, Tony Maxwell, Cynthia Nelson, Rebecca Odes, Tim Orr, Billy Reeves, and Benjamin Wheelock. Thanks also to Suzie Barnes for help with scheduling, Steve Shelley for fact-checking, and Michael Corn, Hugh Flynn, Cynthia Nelson, Tim Orr, and Jesse and Luke once again for supplying archival material such as photos, flyers, reviews, and recordings.

CHAPTER NOTES

1: Whatever happened to you on that street?
Morry, Emily. "Roots: Rochester's Elite Enjoyed Council Rock." *Democrat & Chronicle*, May 19, 2016.

Fabricant, Florence. "Dining Out." *New York Times*, December 11, 1977.

Hartman, Susan. "For a Few Rock Players, Music Is All in the Family." *New York Times*, September 8, 1988.

Coveleski, Stan. National Baseball Hall of Fame. https://baseballhall.org/hall-of-famers/coveleski-stan.

Hell, Richard. *I Dreamed I Was a Very Clean Tramp: An Autobiography*. Ecco, 2014.

Palmer, Robert. *Rolling Stone*, September 3, 1992.

Haynes, Todd. "Interview." *Bomb*, October 1, 1995. https://bombmagazine.org/articles/1995/10/01/kelly-reichardt/.

2: Whatever happened to you in that club?
Newman, Melinda. "The Beat." *Billboard*, July 10, 1993.

Jennings, Dave. "A Kind of Majik." *Melody Maker*, December 3, 1994.

"Sammy." *Trouser Press*. https://trouserpress.com/reviews/sammy/.

Scanlon, Ann. *Vox*, August 1994.

Karrion, Kyd. *Raw*, August 3–16, 1994.

True, Everett. "Albums." *Melody Maker*, July 9, 1994.

Cameron, Keith. *New Musical Express*, July 16, 1994.

Miller, Eric T. *Magnet*, July 1994.

Daley, David. *Alternative Press*, May 1995.

True, Everett. "Singles." *Melody Maker*, February 25, 1995.

Nussbaum, Emily. *Cue the Sun!: The Invention of Reality TV*. Random House, 2024.

Stonefield, Erica. "Landing a Big Time Record Deal." *Great Neck Record*, June 20, 1996.

Jennings, Dave. "Albums." *Melody Maker*, July 20, 1996.

Eliscu, Jenny. *CMJ*, April 8, 1996.

Goldsmith, Mike. *New Musical Express*, June 1, 1996.

Mills, Fred. *Puncture*, no. 36.

Christgau, Robert. "Consumer Guide." *Village Voice*, July 23, 1996.

LaPorte, Nicole. *The Men Who Would Be King: An Almost Epic Tale of Moguls, Movies, and a Company Called DreamWorks*. Mariner Books, 2018.

3: Whatever happened to your old guitar?
Ross, Beck. *Melody Maker*, November 7, 2000.

Long, April. *New Musical Express*, June 9, 2001.

Fletcher, Tony. *New York Newsday*, April 19, 2001.

Taylor, J. R. "Music." *New York Press*, October 10–16, 2001.

Alternative Press, May 2001.

Cancy, Michael. "No Money Mo' Problems: Pitkin's Closes Down." *Village Voice*, October 22, 2007.

Price, Simon. "The Joy of Segues—with Osmonds as Dessert." *The Independent*, August 12, 2001.

www.ingramcontent.com/pod-product-compliance
Lightning Source LLC
LaVergne TN
LVHW041920070526
838199LV00051BA/2678